£ 2-45

IDEAS FOR INTERESTING GARDENS

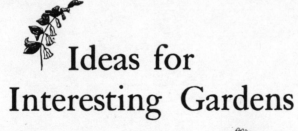

Ideas for Interesting Gardens

DAPHNE MORE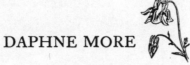

with 6 colour plates, 12
pages of black and white photographs
and drawings by the author

DAVID & CHARLES

NEWTON ABBOT · LONDON · NORTH POMFRET (VT)

To my mother,
who loved gardens

0 7153 6445 6

© Daphne More 1974

Set in 11 on 13 point Baskerville and printed in
Great Britain by W J Holman Limited
for David & Charles (Holdings) Limited
South Devon House Newton Abbot Devon

Contents

List of Illustrations

Acknowledgements

My thanks are due to the photographers who took the pictures for this book, in particular to Mr E. C. O'Brien, Mr J. E. Tiffin and Mr F. G. Vernon who went to considerable trouble on my behalf; also to Captain E. J. Tredwell, late–CBI for Hampshire, who read the bee chapter and made helpful comments; also to my son Jonathan for bearing with me during the writing.

Photographs by—E. C. O'Brien: plates 1, 2 (left), 3, 6, 7, 9 (bottom), 12; colour plates 2, 3. J. E. Tiffin: plates 4, 5. F. G. Vernon: plates 8, 9 (top). H. Smith: plates 10, 11; colour plate 4 (top). A-Z Collection: plate 2 (right). L. H. Newman: colour plate 4 (bottom). Alfieri: colour plate 1.

Chapter 1

Gardens Are for Enjoyment

WHETHER a garden is interesting or not depends on who is looking at it. One person's passion is another person's yawn. To me, an interesting garden must have something different about it, some special quality or extra dimension which distinguishes it from other gardens. It may be the variety of wildlife it supports, the restfulness of its atmosphere, or the unusual way in which plants are used to produce a certain effect. It may be that it is planned around some hobby—collecting old-fashioned plants or growing fruit, keeping bees or breeding goldfish—and this is what gives it a unique character.

When gardens were large and tended by hired labour, it was reasonable to have lawns and flower-beds and rockeries, a peach house, orchards and topiary, a rose-garden, an iris-garden, a kitchen-garden, a rhododendron walk, an avenue of beeches and anything else which came to mind. It is my belief that the owner had most of it because it was 'the done thing', but there was probably one particular aspect which he really enjoyed and took a personal interest in. Perhaps he was inordinately proud of his dahlias or his grapes. Perhaps he liked to spend time sitting in some sunny corner sprinkling crumbs for the fish in a sky-reflecting pool. Perhaps his spirits lifted at sight of his fine trees. Perhaps he secretly thought the primrose-scented path through his wild garden was worth acres of shaven lawn and formal flower-beds. Gardening has many

9

faces and there cannot be a person alive who would not find
pleasure in at least one of them. Today, when gardens are
smaller, sometimes very small indeed, we cannot afford space
for even a little bit of everything, though some people do try.
It is better to choose one aspect of gardening which appeals to
you and pursue that with all you have. It may seem obvious
but it is surprising how few people start a garden by honestly
considering what they *really* like and would look after.

A garden should be more than something to keep your
neighbours at a reasonable distance, more than somewhere to
park the car or hang the washing or turn out the kids when
they get on your nerves. It can—and should—give a tremendous
return, not in terms of money but of pleasure and well-being.
It can be a place for studying nature or playing games like
croquet or clock golf, a source of materials for the flower-
arranger, of subjects for the painter or photographer, or of
unusual vegetables and herbs for the cook; even a setting for a
collection of pieces of modern sculpture.

If a person has an overwhelming interest in growing a
certain kind of plant—orchids or chrysanthemums, for instance
—his choice is easy. He will buy a suitable greenhouse and
leave the rest of his garden as grass with a tree or two to
relieve the monotony. Such specialist interests are time-
consuming, and with visits to shows and famous collections
tend to leave little leisure for anything else. At the other end
of the scale are people, non-gardeners almost, who do not want
to acquire any technical expertise but who enjoy watching
wild birds and butterflies and would like to encourage them;
or those who simply want a peaceful, leafy, undemanding place
for reading or eating out on fine days. It is too easy to settle for
a conventional arrangement of lawn, paths and flower-beds
without consulting your individual tastes and way of life, and
this results in stereotyped gardens which are a chore and a bore.

Many people today have more calls on their time and more
varied interests than ever before, so I have concentrated on
gardens which are easy to look after. Planning a garden round

one basic idea usually results in a simple, cohesive layout which is both more effective and more labour-saving than a confusion of rather indefinite features. Retired people who are making a new garden or modifying an old one for easier working should find the suggestions as useful as will working couples with limited free time.

It is wise to consider other hobbies and amusements in deciding what sort of garden you want. For instance, if the whole family consists of sailing enthusiasts who spend every leisure moment afloat, there is not much point in planning a garden as a riot of summer flowers. It will be a riot of weeds and deadheads whenever anyone is there to see it. A garden of grass and conifers which would be unusual and as attractive in winter as in summer, might be a better notion. In case this sounds very dull and limited, I must mention that there are at least eighty forms of *Chamaecyparis*, the family to which the well-known Lawson's cypress belongs. They come in all sizes and a fantastic variety of shapes, weeping and with twisted branchlets, prostrate and spraying out like ferns, as well as the conical and bun-shaped ones; and the colours include sulphur-yellow, bronze, grey, blue, white-tipped and several shades of green ranging from lime to near-black. That is just one family. There are also cedars, pines, firs and 'monkey-puzzles', junipers and yews in endless variety. Dwarf conifers alone run into dozens. A most attractive garden could be made using only these, perhaps with heathers for ground-cover while the conifers are developing, and it would need little attention.

Then, too, it is a good idea to look ahead. Do you plan to have a family, which may mean less—or more—free time and call for a different sort of garden? Do you expect to move in a year or two? I knew a man with a passion for alpines. Perhaps because he was a very large man, the Lilliputian perfection of these tiny flowers fascinated him. He laid out a magnificent rock garden in his small plot, knowing that promotion in his firm would entail moving, and then was torn with indecision when his chance came. Had he paved or grassed his garden

and grown his alpines in a variety of tubs and troughs and
sinks, he could have taken them to his new home and avoided
the agonies.

This is a book of ideas, not a gardening manual. There are
already hundreds of excellent publications covering all the
technical side of gardening. Others deal comprehensively with
a specific subject, and some of these giving further information
about topics in this book are listed in the Appendix. Most of
the books can be borrowed from public libraries, but if you
develop an interest in a particular aspect of gardening you will
probably want to buy a reliable reference book. I have tried
to avoid giving long lists of plants, while being careful to
mention those which are valuable for specific purposes and
situations. A few people are put off by Greek and Latin names,
but we cannot do without them altogether: many plants have
no common name, or the common name covers several related
ones. The full botanical description is necessary if you are to
get the exact plant you want from the nursery. A reference list
of common names and their botanical equivalents is given at
the end of this book, to avoid repetition.

Here and there I have suggested less common, and neglected,
plants and trees. These may not be available in garden centres
and department stores which tend to sell a restricted range of
mass-produced plants, thereby contributing to the sameness
one notices in many modern gardens. It is worth looking farther
afield for something different. At a time when people increasingly live in similar houses, wear similar clothes, use
similar kitchen equipment and so on, it is refreshing to have
gardens which are entirely individual. The catalogues of
specialist nurseries (which advertise in gardening magazines)
are full of information, though their descriptions are sometimes
over-ecstatic. Some are beautifully illustrated and well worth
the few pence you may have to pay for them. Many nurseries
can be visited, and gardens which are open to the public offer
another way of increasing one's 'plant vocabulary'—those in
your own district give a guide to what will thrive in your soil

and conditions. Booklets giving addresses and the dates when gardens are on view are listed in the Appendix. In some gardens all the plants are labelled, but if not there is usually somebody who is only too happy to tell you the name of something which catches your eye.

The garden begins with a plot of ground which may be large or small, crammed with all the time-devouring features essential to Victorian householders (probably in a state of dire neglect) or bare of anything except waste concrete, broken bricks, and mounds of intractable subsoil; it may be swept by cold winds, or be boggy, gloomy or sunbaked, flat or precipitous. What are we going to do with it? We have first to think about its assets and its disadvantages, about the house it surrounds, and about ourselves: what time we propose to spend in it, our tastes and amusements and future prospects, whether we are obsessively tidy or have a more permissive attitude, whether we find wildlife interesting or regard birds as a noisy nuisance.

Some books give detailed plans for laying out and planting gardens, but unfortunately the piece of ground available very rarely matches the drawing; its proportions are different or the house faces east not south. Thus the roses end up in shade not sun, and the herb bed is overshadowed by the beech tree next door. Any sketches I give are purposely vague, showing only an idea which can be adapted to fit actual conditions. It is not possible to produce plans which could be used on every site, and how dull if it were! Each garden must be a unique creation, though this does not mean that ideas cannot be taken from plans or pictures or from existing gardens and modified to suit the circumstances.

The work involved in planning and making a new garden can be made easier if you are realistic about the kind of garden you want and are prepared to begin with a simple scheme and let it develop. Too many people start with an elaborate idea which they have neither the time nor the energy to carry out properly, and sooner or later they give up in despair. You must also be realistic about the plot. Trying to grow herbs which demand sunlight and good drainage in a city backyard shaded by tall buildings is unrealistic: the result will always be disappointing however much effort you put in. Make the best of what you have. A high blank wall can be an asset, intelligently used, and a steep slope can be exploited rather than laboriously levelled, which in any case might spoil the drainage. If yours is a chalky soil, stop hankering after azaleas and instead plant flowering cherries and Japanese quince, lilacs and clematis, which will thrive in it. Fighting nature is exhausting and profitless.

Two points to watch are scale and suitability. A design which looks splendid in a castle garden is unlikely to suit a suburban one-tenth of an acre without radical alteration. Some schemes just cannot be scaled down successfully, though it may be possible to achieve a similar *effect* using smaller and fewer plants. I remember a small corner site in which the owner had tried to reproduce the peaceful atmosphere of a circular, evergreen-enclosed garden seen at some stately home. He had laid his grass and girdled it with *Cupressus*, quite forgetting the size of the original plot. In a few years his conifers shut out all the light and the result more nearly resembled the bottom of a well than the spacious and sunny amphitheatre he had had in his mind's eye. But there was nothing wrong with the idea: carried out with more suitable evergreens it could have succeeded. Scale is just as important in the relationship between the various components of a garden. Special features need to be large enough to make an impact, but not so large that they dominate everything else. To take an extreme example, you *could* get away with having a large tree in a small garden if there were nothing else except uncluttered grass and/or paving; but not in conjunction with small flower-beds and little winding paths. This assumes an established tree which it would be a crime to fell: for present planting one would choose something of more suitable size. Or one hopes so! We tend to be unrealistic about growth, happily planting a nice little shrub which will block all the light from the sitting-room window in three years' time, or a tree which will become a menace to passing buses if it is not lopped.

Suitability also means studying the style of the house and choosing the kind of garden features which blend with, and enhance, it. Broadly speaking, I mean that 'olde-worlde' wells and rustic garden furniture do not consort happily with flat-roofed contemporary-style bungalows; that crazy paving and oak five-barred gates add nothing to the dignity and elegance of Georgian or neo-Georgian houses; that a stone fountain with Tritons is too grand for a spruced-up country cottage; and that a medieval-type lych-gate makes a bizarre approach to a yellow brick semi (or anything else). Plants and trees are almost universally acceptable but an ill-chosen style of gates and paving, seats, paths, summer-houses and garden ornaments can strike a very discordant note. Sometimes the surprising can be very effective: I remember with enormous pleasure the spiky bronze Don Quixote encountered in the lush floweriness of an English cottage garden. It was only later that I reflected what an odd choice this was; at the time the romantic figure had a magical inevitability which is hard to explain.

There is no need to strain after absolute accuracy in style or materials; it is a matter of sympathy, of similar mood. For instance, finding genuine Tudor pots to stand in the courtyard of a timber-framed cottage would be impossible, but wooden tubs or simple terracotta pots, large flowerpots or the bread-crock type of thing, would fit in better than a fibreglass reproduction of an Italian lead urn. The formal symmetry of a Georgian-style house might seem to call for a formal geometric garden, with a straight path to the front door between clipped box hedges and so on. Formal gardens need constant attention because neatness is their primary quality, but one can compromise by having a formal layout with less demanding plants, ie the straight path to the door, but edged with lavender and not box so that it requires trimming only once a year. The effect is similar but not so rigid. However, this type of house can be married even to a wild sort of garden, certainly to a quite informal one, if there is a link area close to the building such as a terrace with pots or a surround of plain, close-cut lawn, giving way to rougher grass, trees and shrubs beyond. Climbers on the house also help to unite them.

Perhaps the most difficult part of planning a garden is knowing where to begin, even when you have decided on a basic theme and know the sort of general effect you want. If there is an established tree on the ground, this can be a starting point. Do you see it as the end of a vista? Could it be paired with another to frame some interesting feature farther on? Would it be ideal for giving shade to one end of a sitting-out area? If one of your priorities is a terrace or stretch of paving, begin by deciding where it should be. It is customary to tack it on to the back of the house, irrespective of which way it faces, but the best place might be halfway down one side of the plot or at the far end. You will then want a path to it from the house, and a plan at once begins to take shape. Do not start with a path: paths should always go somewhere, and it is advisable to decide first where they are going. The most direct way is usually the best. This does not mean that the path should not curve. Paths twisting out of sight have a particular attraction in a wild sort of garden, but there should be something to give the bend a reason for being there—a large shrub, a bank covered with daffodils, or a tree stump, so that people will not simply cut across it. Meaningless wriggles are irritating and fussy. If you are in doubt, the simplest plan is always best. Another starting point might be the screening of an eyesore beyond your boundary. What would be the best thing to plant there, bearing in mind the central theme of your garden-to-be? It may be that the theme will itself provide the starting point: there may be only one suitable place for a pond or for apple trees, and you can go on from there.

But first of all, what is going to make your garden interesting? The ideas I shall put forward in subsequent chapters are not meant to be followed slavishly. Much depends on personal inclination and the size and situation of the plot. You may be

Easily-maintained garden of grass, daffodils and trees

(*left*) Woodruff, a pretty carpet under trees

(*right*) Foxgloves, a natural for woodland

introduced to a kind of garden you have never previously considered, or be persuaded to take a new and appreciative look at wild flowers or birds or the stranger examples of plant life. I suggest some possibilities but there are many more, and gardens have a way of evolving. The flowery grass described in one chapter could develop into the informal fruit garden dealt with elsewhere. The owner of a large garden devoted to grass and trees might like to enclose a sheltered, restful corner near the house and fill it with scented plants and seating. Someone whose simply planned garden leaves him plenty of free time may choose to explore the mysteries of bee-keeping. Doves or goldfish might add a further dimension of interest in almost any garden, or it might be transformed into a safe and amusing playground for small children. My hope is that readers will pick out any ideas which strike them as interesting, and use them as a basis for making their own individual and really enjoyable gardens.

B

Chapter 2

Mainly Grass

ABOUT the most undemanding way of using a plot of ground is by growing grass. There is something as reposeful about unbroken stretches of grass as there is about calm water. A well-proportioned house or really distinguished bungalow is shown to advantage in a grass setting, but it needs a squarish plot so that there is space at both sides of the house as well as at front and back. If the house is an ugly duckling this kind of treatment will accentuate its faults, though the addition of climbers and some well-sited trees may work wonders. A modern house of unusual or advanced design often blends successfully with a background of close-cut grass, but where a building has long low lines the contrast of one or two important trees is needed to avoid monotony and lift the eye. Builders sometimes leave mature trees on sites these days, at least on the smaller developments, and if a new householder is fortunate enough to acquire a copper beech or a group of silver birches, grass may be all that is needed to show off both trees and house. A paved area round the building, not necessarily symmetrical in shape, and some shrubs in pots or well-trained climbers on the walls, will act as a link between house and garden to the advantage of both.

There is a certain formality about a close-cut lawn which makes it a good setting for a formal, symmetrical style of house, but other features should be in character. Crazy paving, for instance, would be out of place and coloured slabs tend to look cheap. Rectangular paving stones are best for paths and terraces, though gravel, well rolled and neatly confined at the edges, can look nice. Unfortunately it tends to scatter into the grass, grows weeds, and is sometimes uncomfortable to walk on. The technique of spraying with tar and surfacing with gravel produces a similar appearance without these drawbacks. Tarmac seems to me to be a most unsympathetic material in any garden. In a formal setting clipped hedges are more appropriate than wooden fences or woven panels, since the cost of walling is nowadays prohibitive. Electric clippers reduce the time spent in maintaining them, but even so, long hedges are best made from something which requires less attention than time-honoured privet, box, hawthorn or *Lonicera nitida*.

Holly will manage with a yearly trim because it grows slowly, but it may take ten years to reach a satisfactory size. Beech and hornbeam are alternatives, and both keep their leaves, though in brown-papery form, until the new ones start unfolding in spring. Beech (*Fagus sylvatica*) or its purple form (*F.s. purpurea*) will grow to 4ft in four years, put into good soil at 12in high, but will only need clipping in August once it is established. For the first two years do not clip it at all; then only trim the sides lightly in July until the required height is reached. Hornbeam (*Carpinus betulus*) also needs only a light July trim until it is established, then a quite severe one each August. It makes a dense hedge to 10ft high. The two popular laurels (*Prunus laurocerasus* and *P. lusitanica*) will do well in sun or shade and in any soil, and will manage with a trimming each July. Ideally this should be done with secateurs to avoid cutting and spoiling the big leaves, but this is hardly practicable where a long hedge needs attention. Yew (*Taxus baccata*) makes a splendid evergreen hedge where there is room, but it looks heavy in a small garden. The foliage is poisonous to cattle and horses so yew must never be planted where a paddock or pasture adjoins the garden. *Cupressus macrocarpa* is sometimes used for hedging but it dislikes being clipped: one or two trees will often die or turn brown at the base which looks most unattractive. Lawson's cypress (*Chamaecyparis lawsoniana*) is also intolerant of clipping. If a conifer hedge is wanted, *Thuya plicata* is quick-growing and tolerates a clip in late summer. A white-painted fence of the 'ranch-board' type does not look out of place as an alternative to hedging, where privacy is not a consideration. It would need regular repainting but it is not a fiddly job to do.

All this presupposes a fairly spacious plot, but today the frontage is usually narrow even though the garden may go back a long way. The house and garage effectively cut the garden into two, a small piece in front and a larger area behind. A long, narrow back garden does not lend itself to uninterrupted lawn. The eye travelling down its length seems to draw in the side boundaries, making it seem still longer and narrower, like a road. Some division is needed to break the length, which will have the effect of increasing the apparent width. A change of level across the plot, with two or three steps up or down, will make a great difference. If there is a bank between the levels the mower will not be impeded. The steps need not be in the middle. Another idea is to make a generous paved area right across the far end of the plot for sitting-out, preferably reached by a few steps, and furnished with some pleasant seats and a table. This is particularly good if the house itself faces south, so that a terrace adjoining the back of it would always be in shade. The long narrow plot could also be divided by means of a hedge in which an archway or opening gives a view into the farther part. The two parts of the dividing hedge need not be opposite each other, nor the opening in the middle, nor the two 'rooms' of similar size. Treatment of the separate areas could be quite different: the farther one might be less formal, or planned as an orchard or kitchen-garden.

If a close-cut lawn is to be the main focus of attention it needs to be good: this means regular mowing, rolling, feeding and weed-control. Given mechanical aids the work is not too arduous, and many people think it worth while. However, such a lawn is not in itself interesting, though it may be a

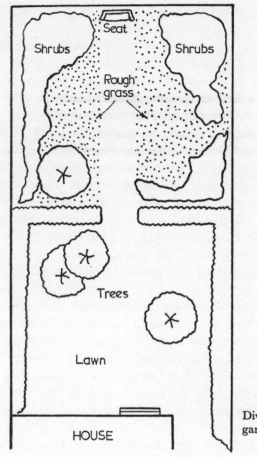

Seat

Shrubs   Shrubs

Rough grass

Trees

Lawn

HOUSE

Dividing a long narrow garden into 'rooms'

marvellous background for something which is—a beautiful house, some pieces of sculpture or a formal pool full of lilies and exotic fish. A perfect lawn demands respect. It should not be walked on when wet, or cluttered up with summer-houses and sand-pits, or have tent pegs and cricket stumps hammered into it. It might be used for a decorous game of croquet but not for football. Some of my best friends are children and dogs and I would prefer to have at least some grass that they too can enjoy. Rough grass. This is likely to become increasingly popular because it is undemanding and can be much more interesting.

Longer grass is informal and does not go with trimmed hedges and straight paved paths, or indeed with some houses. More formal types of house need a wide terrace and possibly an area of lawn beyond that before the rougher grass takes over. Pleasant effects can be obtained by contrasting long and short grass, as for instance where closely mown paths run through longer, flower-patterned grass. Curving lines where the different textures meet can be used to distract the eye from corners and soften the rectangular shape of most plots. If a house has been built on old pasture, this can often be improved by levelling the hollows and cutting frequently with a rotary mower, which will eliminate most of the ranker weeds. In any case, expensive soil-preparation and first-class turves are not necessary. Rotovating, rolling and grass-seed will produce an adequate turf.

Daffodils always look their best in grass, but they are a nuisance in a proper lawn because the foliage should be left to die naturally. This means that odd areas must be left uncut for weeks. Moreover, turf which has been regularly mown and rolled becomes so compacted that few plants will thrive in it. In rough grass daffodils show their satisfaction by increasing and looking lovelier every year, and dying leaves are comparatively unobtrusive.

Rough grass can be cut as often as inclination allows, but a multitude of flowers will flourish in it if cutting is carefully timed and limited to three times a year. The result may be meadowlike at times but the area will be rich in wildlife, not only grasshoppers and butterflies and suchlike but possibly also slow-worms and hedgehogs, voles, shrews and dormice. Some people have a hazy notion that this would lead to mice invading their homes, but the house-mouse is a different creature altogether. Shrews, for instance, live on insects and would never find enough for their needs indoors, while voles lay up winter stores of seeds and berries underground and scorn to enter houses. This kind of grass must not be treated with selective weedkillers, nor any manures or fertilisers which will cause some plants to grow rapidly at the expense of others. If you can scythe it, the long swathes are aesthetically more pleasing than the chopped-up residue of the rotary mower. Good scythe-men are scarce but there is something therapeutic about practising this ancient skill. If a mower is used the blades should be set high.

In my grassland it is a toss-up whether a snowdrop or a crocus appears first in the year. Snowdrops are naturally woodland plants and tend to diminish rather than increase when competing with grass. The large-flowered Dutch hybrid crocuses are another matter. More and more come up cheerfully each year and their long-lasting foliage is hidden by the growing grass. Some of the species crocuses flower before the Dutch ones and increase quickly where conditions suit them, notably *C. tomasinianus* (blue) and mauve-striped *C. imperati*. They are best not mixed with the Dutch ones which look blowsy by comparison.

Daffodils and narcissi come next, though in fact all are really narcissi. Mixed bulbs for naturalising are cheap, flower well after the first year and multiply quickly. They are generally the larger kind but it would be a pity to leave out the small daffodil called the Lent lily (*Narcissus pseudonarcissus*) which begins to open in late February. The Hoop Petticoat daffodil (*Bulbocodium conspicuus*) is also delightful. These do better in light soils where the grasses are less rank. The heavy damp soil they dislike is more suited to the Snakeshead fritillary, *Fritillaria meleagris*. These Sullen Ladies, as they are sometimes called, are thought sinister-looking by some people, but to my mind they are altogether enchanting. Sometimes the hanging bells are pure white, but normally they are purple-chequered and grow about 6in tall. Where conditions suit them they will spread into a dark carpet of flowers.

Violets often seed themselves and will flower freely in grass, especially under deciduous trees. Primroses too will thrive, though they do not make big lush plants unless they are in partial shade. The many-coloured polyanthus also flowers quite well. On chalkland cowslips will flourish and hybridise with primroses and polyanthuses to produce varied offspring.

Snakeshead fritillary,
Fritillaria meleagris

Bluebells follow the daffodils. The true bluebell likes shady woodland conditions but the larger, stronger kind known as the Spanish hyacinth (*Scilla campanulata*) does just as well in grassland. The flowers are various shades of mauve, blue and lilac-pink as well as white and they increase quickly. All bulbs should be planted, not in lines and circles around trees, but haphazardly, so that they form natural-looking drifts.

In May, natural grassland resembles the flowery fields depicted in medieval tapestries. Wild flowers establish themselves: ox-eye daisies, clovers, meadow-cranesbill, speedwells and campions, poppies, pink and white dead-nettles, dandelions, lady's-smock, mallow and cow-parsley. These—and the wild grasses—feed the caterpillars of those characteristic meadow butterflies, the Blues and Small Copper, Speckled Wood, Heath, Gatekeeper and Marbled White, the Clouded Yellow and Meadow Brown. Except for one or two species, butterflies are becoming rare in gardens, and as selective weed-killers continue to eliminate their food-plants from pasture and road verges they will become rarer still. By giving a home to these wild flowers you can enjoy the wildlife which they support. Docks and thistles I would try to control, but the others can grow as they will. The wild wood anemone will sometimes establish itself in shady grass and the colourful de Caen anemone often does surprisingly well. Grape hyacinth is another bulbous plant whose foliage looks shabby in a flower-bed but is lost in grass. Its splendid blue contrasts well with the white and green of the Star of Bethlehem, *Ornithogalum umbellatum*, and its relative *O. nutans*. Both these are apt to become weeds in cultivated ground but are pretty and well-behaved in grass. I would even include tulips though they are considered unsuitable for naturalising. The flowers are smaller but to my eye look happier in grass than standing evenly spaced in a cloud of forget-me-nots. Incidentally, forget-me-nots also often thrive in grass.

In May most of the grasses flower and are very pretty too, if you are not a martyr to hay fever. The first cut of the year in early June will lay them low and the stalks will look drab for a week or two until the new green, and quick-blooming wild flowers spring up again. By the end of August another cut will be needed before the colchicums or autumn crocuses come through. They are called Naked Ladies because the flowers come before the leaves, but they look less nude in grass. *C. speciosum* does especially well and may still be out in October. When its flowers fade the grass should be cut for the third and last time, for their leaves will not appear until spring. This is a good time to sprinkle some hardy annual seeds on any bare patches—such as where you have dug out a huge dock—to give you a few pleasant surprises next year. A packet of Children's Garden Mixture can be thinly distributed, or any left-overs if you have grown annuals in pots on the terrace.

This interesting tapestry of grass and flowers is best enclosed with shrubs. A wooden fence may be needed to confine children or dogs but wire mesh is less expensive and just as efficient and would be hidden by the shrubs in three years. I have used the

strong cheap fencing called pig-wire for this, though the square
mesh tempts children to climb it. Where the only need is to
mark the boundary, posts and wires would do.

Since unclipped shrubs take up more room than a hedge
does, do not plant them too close to the boundary. Allow for
their being 5–6ft through eventually. Where something tall
needs screening, a neighbour's garage for instance, put in a
tree or group of trees, or a shrub which will quickly reach
7–8ft. A group of Lawson's cypress, or one of the laurels would
do this, and both are evergreen. Laurel left to grow naturally
will reach 20ft eventually and bears attractive racemes of
cream-coloured flowers. Privet is another inexpensive shrub
which grows to a good height if left alone, and produces
flowers and attractive black berries. Golden privet is especially
worth while as the leaves always look sunny, and are as

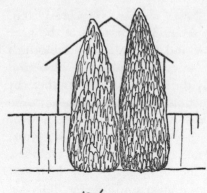

Screening with conifers and
deciduous trees

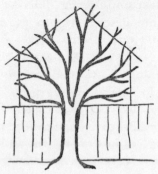

effective a contrast to green foliage as the choicest variegated shrubs.

A conifer is not always the best choice for screening an ugly building, as it tends to be narrow at the top. A small deciduous tree, a purple prunus, whitebeam, hawthorn or crab-apple with a rounded head may do the job more effectively in summer, and even in winter the tracery of branches will break up the lines of the building, making it much less obtrusive. Incidentally, make sure that your tree will actually screen the eyesore. It is not just a matter of planting it beside the building; it must be between the building and the place you see it from. For instance, if you plant your tree so that the ugly shed is screened when you look from your sitting-room window, it will still be all too visible from your sitting-out place at the bottom of the

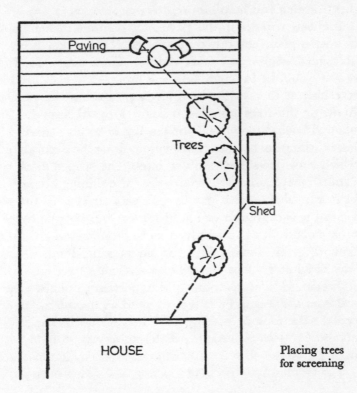

Placing trees
for screening

garden. Two or three trees or tall shrubs may be needed to exclude it completely. The thing to do is to stick a beanpole or something similar into the ground and then go and study it from your vantage point, visualising the shape of the tree's head and making sure that it would in fact screen the eyesore.

One very quick-growing and effective shrub for screening is *Buddleia globosa*. This is not the September-flowering *B. davidii* with purple plumes on long arching branches, but a more solid shrub bearing little balls of orange flowers in June. The foliage is greyish, and evergreen in all but very severe winters, and the shrub will soon reach its maximum of 8–10ft high and as much through. Forsythia, *Berberis darwinii*, lilac, the dogwoods like *Cornus alba* and its variegated form *Spaethii*, and rhododendrons (if the soil suits) are other large-growing shrubs which will help blot out unwelcome sights.

It is better to group this perimeter planting rather than put in single plants of different species. Twos and threes with occasional singles look more natural. On a large plot fives or sevens would be in scale. Where a group of trees is needed for screening or to vary the line, lower shrubs may be planted in front, or the trees may be brought forward and the shrubs planted behind to conceal the fencing or to give privacy. The latter arrangement is useful for emphasising the decorative bark which some trees have: silver birch, the striped bark of the Chinese maple, *Acer grosseri hersii*, or the shining coppery bark of *Prunus serrula*. Birch trunks look very striking in the winter against a background of laurel leaves, and by planting them on a mound they can be given more prominence. An artificial mound, gently sloping into the surrounding land, is a quick way of adding a foot or two to a screening tree, and will use soil removed in excavation. It is important to remove the topsoil from the area to be raised, to build up the mound and then replace the topsoil, adding dead leaves, lawn-mowings, peat and other moisture-retaining materials as you proceed, because higher ground will naturally dry out quicker than the level.

For an informal effect, the rectangular shape of the average

plot will need concealing. This means letting the perimeter
planting surge forward in a peninsula here and there, and
rounding off the far corners, but not symmetrically. It is a
good idea to arrange a space behind a corner planting where
prunings can be burnt and cut grass rotted down in a compost

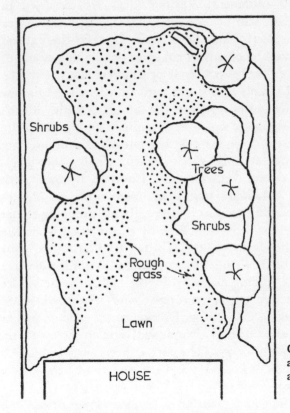

Contrasting long
and short grass in
an informal setting

pit, though grass-mowings could also be applied as a mulch
round the roots of shrubs which prefer a cool damp root-run.
Do not put these on thickly as they heat up and could be
harmful. On a long narrow plot the shrubs could be brought
forward on both sides to form peninsulas, but not opposite
each other. This gives a tantalising glimpse of the farther
garden while minimising the roadway effect of the narrow plot.

Avoid too many curves and indentations, however, or the result will be fussy and artificial.

This sort of garden lures one on to see what is hidden at the far end, and there should be something to satisfy the explorer. It does not need to be anything elaborate—just a seat or a pool or some suitable ornament. Various ideas are discussed in Chapter 9. A path will be needed to this point since longer grass dries more slowly than lawn does. To keep the natural look the path could be of closely cut grass or stepping-stones of irregular shape, either broken stone or concrete cast in situ. To do this, the turf should be cut out with sufficient soil to allow at least a 2in thickness of concrete, the top being flush with the ground to let the mower run over it without harm. Tamp the earth in the bottom down hard before putting in and levelling the mix. Fine concrete mix which contains small stones is less slippery than a smooth cement finish. Cover each 'stone' with an opened-out polythene bag held down with pebbles to prevent it from drying too fast and crumbling. Stepping-stones can be made two or three at a time by this method when the weather and other factors allow. To decide the route of your path, walk two or three times from your house to the objective and mark where you go, allowing for the later increase in size of any shrub or tree you have to go round. The chances are that you will get an easy curve. Do not be tempted to put in extra bends for artistic effect. People will only cut across them. Putting stepping-stones too far apart is a common fault. An elderly lady of 5ft 2in does not have the same stride as a healthy 6ft male!

If grass and informal planting is to extend right from the house, climbers on the walls will help to link house and garden, but they should be the kind which does not demand rigid training or clipping: roses, clematis, jasmine, honeysuckle and *Garrya elliptica* come to mind. An area of paving is popular for outdoor meals, for sitting out and playing on, because it is easily kept clean and soon dries after rain. This also forms a link between house and garden if style and material are well-chosen. For instance, there is no need for the paving to have a straight edge or to be symmetrical in shape. It could be wider at the end which catches the sun for longer, or it could bulge out into the grass; but keep the shape simple and bold rather than complicated. Paving needs to be in keeping with the house, and also with the stepping-stones if these are used. Do not overlook the possibility of mixing materials. I have seen bricks and areas of concrete brushed to expose the aggregate used effectively together. Gaps may be left for low-growing plants but choose these carefully. Fleshy houseleeks (*Sempervivums*) get kicked to pieces whereas creeping thymes are unaffected if trodden on; but the latter attract bees when in flower and would not be a good choice if small children crawl about on the paving. Planting should be kept to the edges and out of the main thoroughfare, and limited. It is maddening to find that by opening the French window you behead a clump of Mrs Sinkins pinks, and that you cannot put up a folding table without squashing something else.

Once established this garden will allow plenty of time for enjoying it without the guilty knowledge that hedges want clipping, edges need trimming and weeds are sullying the bare soil of the rose-beds. Whether it is visually interesting when there are no flowers in the grass depends largely on the choice of shrubs, their contrasting flower and leaf shapes, colours, habits of growth and so on. Plants can be tall, arching, feathery, dense, spiky, billowing, cushion-shaped, sprawling or pyramidal. There may be flowers in spires or balls or clusters or singly, like stars or saucers or bells, and in a huge range of colours. Leaves may be grey, brown, purple, yellow, red, white or very different shades of green, and be of any size, shape and texture—long, round, dissected, ferny, leathery, downy, rough or shiny. It is up to you to make a selection which will please you individually and form a constantly changing but always interesting picture.

Chapter 3

Woodland Glades

A GOOD MANY people do not really like gardens that are neat and orderly, with overtones of hard work, but most people like woods if they are not too dense. So instead of packing kids, sandwiches and leaky thermos flasks into the car and setting off in search of a delightful woodland glade, why not create one in the back garden?

This is really a development of the shrub-bordered grassy garden which was discussed at the end of Chapter 2. Wild gardens have been a feature of some stately homes for a long time, but even in a typical suburban back garden, say 40ft × 65ft, it is possible to achieve that effect. To me, a 'wild' garden is suggestive of nettles, briars and other injurious things fighting for survival in dank undergrowth. I prefer 'woodland', because what we want to create is either the ideal sunny clearing with ferns and bluebells under the trees (something one discovers in nature about once in a lifetime), or else a mysterious path winding away out of sight of the house, opening up changing patterns of tree-form, flower and leaf, and leading to—what? One would have to go to see. And there should be something to reward one at the end. In a slightly larger garden it would be possible to have a return path, if only of the narrowest size, to bring one back a different way.

The perimeter of the plot would first have to be screened in the same way as the meadow garden. Holly, hawthorn, privet, Myrobalan plum, laurel, Lawson's cypress, hazel and any

(*above*) Contrasting evergreen leaves: hebe,
rhododendron and silvery
Lamb's Lugs

(*right*) Gardener's Garters
lighten a dull corner

(*left*) Thrush on nest incubating eggs

(*right*) Babies, like this young starling, do *not* need rescuing

number of inexpensive plants can be used for this purpose, putting in two or three together. At first some pruning would be needed to ensure bushiness and to persuade them in the way they should go. Later treatment would be confined to the occasional removal of a dead, awkwardly placed or overlong branch, so that the plants are controlled but keep the natural look.

Besides masking the boundary, these plants can form the basis for happy combinations of plant material. Against tall evergreens the graceful shape of a Young's weeping birch would show to advantage, with a carpet of wild cyclamen at its base. Other planting can be arranged so that this charming picture is suddenly revealed as you walk along your woodland path—a kind of side vista. Woods have this quality of mystery; each twist of the path opens up a fresh view. This is how you must plan your special effects or special plants. There may be a group of *Mahonia aquifolium* beside the path. This shrub grows about 3ft tall and has clustered yellow flowers in March. In autumn the hollylike leaves turn red and bronze but do not fall off. Between whiles the bushes are not so interesting, but if a gap has been left in the group the dark shiny foliage could frame perhaps a purple-leafed nut tree (*Corylus maxima Purpurea*) rising from a little knoll covered with the fresh greenery and tiny white flowers of woodruff (*Asperula odorata*); perhaps the sunny glow which is golden-leafed elder (*Sambucus nigra Aurea*) or that splendid variegated shrub *Elaeagnus pungens Maculata*; or perhaps a mass of the tall glimmering spires of pink and white foxgloves, or a pool of primroses shaded by the opening silver-green leaves of a whitebeam. The possibilities are endless and exciting, and the pleasures of playing off various colours, textures and shapes one against the other are infinite. Leaf contrasts are more reliable than flower combinations because leaves last longer, and any quirk in the weather can delay the flowering of a shrub long enough to upset your carefully planned colour effect. However, some of the happiest effects occur by chance and compensate at times for the failure of another scheme.

c

Any natural feature such as a slope or a boggy corner can be exploited, and uneven ground is an asset. If the land can be reshaped slightly, so that it rises gently at one or both sides of the winding path or is banked up a little on the northern side of the glade, this will add enormously to the effect. A length of tree-trunk can be used to retain a bank of earth in a very natural manner. Any established tree should of course be incorporated into the plan: whatever it is, a mature tree is worth five new saplings. It may need careful shaping or thinning. Take off any dead or ugly branches at their base and paint each cut surface to keep out disease spores. Snags look hideous and they sprout in an ugly way. Saw part way through the branch from below, then make another cut downwards to join the first one, otherwise the weight of the branch will break the last piece and rip a length of bark from the trunk, leaving it unsightly. Careful removal of some of the lower branches from an established tree will allow more light and air to penetrate below. Some overlarge trees can be pollarded, ie the trunk is cut straight across at the required height from the ground. It looks horrible at first but in quite a short time new limbs grow to form a nice round head. Limes, willows and sycamores can be treated this way. It is best to reshape trees in the winter when they are dormant: the branches are lighter without their foliage, and the shape of the tree is clearly visible. Even a dead tree of respectable size or a stout stump is an asset providing it is firm in the ground, because ivy or honeysuckle can be grown over it.

Trees should be chosen which are in scale with the size of the plot. This usually means ignoring the woodland giants like oak and ash, beech and sweet chestnut. In gardens of half an acre or more there is room for a few larger trees but not many and not near the house. Kinds to consider will probably include silver birch and its weeping variety, rowan and its relative whitebeam (*Sorbus aria*, especially the variety *Lutescens*), crab-apple (*Malus*), the smaller willows but *not* the giant golden weeping one which needs 50ft each way all to itself, laburnum, cherry, red hawthorn, the weeping willow-leafed pear (*Pyrus salicifolia*), purple filbert, walnut, and the smaller horse-chestnut or buckeye (*Aesculus carnea*). Don't plant too many and bear in mind the probable size of each, and that of your perimeter screen, in seven to ten years' time. A few conifers will give winter form and colour, and their feathery foliage and generally conical shape contrast effectively with round-headed deciduous trees. Again avoid giants like blue cedar and (since you will not clip them) *Cupressocyparis leylandii* and *Thuya plicata*. There are many conifers which reach a maximum of about 20ft. The coloured forms of *Chamaecyparis lawsoniana* such as *Elwoodii*, *Allumii* and *Stewartii* grow much more slowly than the green type. *Juniperus communis hibernica* is a very narrow juniper which takes a long time to reach 6ft. The blue spruce, *Picea pungens glauca*, is a good colour and a reasonable size.

Groups look more natural than single trees dotted about. Silver birches particularly look right in twos or threes. Stag's horn sumach, *Rhus typhina*, often throws up suckers to form a group of little trees, attractive in their differing heights, though some will have to be removed from time to time. This sumach has furry branches and long palmlike leaves which turn to glowing colours in autumn. It is never too big for even the

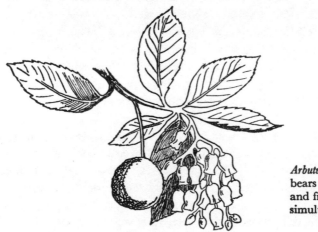

Arbutus unedo
bears flowers
and fruit
simultaneously

smallest garden. Incidentally, it is possible to grow many shrubs on a 'leg' or single trunk to make delightful little trees. I have grown guelder rose this way, removing side shoots up to 4ft from the ground and taking off growths which try to rise from the base. Privet can make a nice little evergreen tree, pruned the same way, and so can many other shrubs more often seen as shapeless bushes—lilac, forsythia, Japanese quince, *Arbutus unedo* (which is evergreen), tamarisk, and several of the cotoneasters such as *simonsii, frigidus* and *watereri*.

Grass is not normal ground-cover in woodland though it will be found in clearings and broad rides where there is more light. There is no reason why your trees should not surround a grassy glade treated like the rough grass discussed in Chapter 2 and planted with bulbs. The trees must not be too close to the house, so an area of grass leading into a grassy path would be a good idea. Thick woodland is mulched with dead leaves and nothing but wood anemones and toadstools grow there, but we are not going to shut out the light in this way and various ground-covering plants—bushes as well as flat carpeters—can be used.

Shrubs which are low-growing and more or less shade-tolerant include February-flowering *Daphne mezereum*, the mahonia already mentioned, skimmia, *Cotoneaster horizontalis*, hardy fuchsias, and the mop-headed *Hortensia* hydrangeas. The spotted laurel, *Aucuba japonica*, also does well in shade and is usually doomed to the darkest spots though it is a cheerful creature if allowed a place in the sun. Hollies will stand a lot of shade and the slow-growing variegated kinds are particularly useful. Where the soil is suitable rhododendrons and azaleas will flourish.

Carpeters are legion and ivy is one of the best, with green and variegated kinds and many different sizes and shapes of foliage. *Lamium galeobdolon*, a kind of dead-nettle with heart-shaped silver-splashed leaves, loops itself about, rooting as it goes. The silver is more pronounced when the plant grows in shade. Its pink-flowered relative, *Lamium maculatum*, is another possibility. The periwinkles have pretty blue flowers. *Vinca minor* is denser and perhaps slightly more effective as a weed-smotherer than *V. major*, but the latter has a very attractive variegated form called *Elegantissima*. All are evergreen. Another dense evergreen growing 12in high is the Rose of Sharon, *Hypericum calycinum*. This has large yellow flowers with a brush of stamens at the centre and will produce them in shade, though I think it flowers more freely on a sunny bank. Elephant's Ears(*Bergenia cordifolia*) is evergreen and weed-suppressing but grows more slowly than the others.

Primroses are a woodland natural, of course. Violets too will thrive and cover the soil. Bulbs like bluebells and corms like the autumn-flowering *Cyclamen neapolitanum* will flourish in drifts under trees. Lilies-of-the-valley produce their dainty bells in April/May but the leaves are long-lasting and the root-mat is very dense. They are sometimes difficult to establish but quite suddenly settle down and increase rapidly, so do not lose heart too soon. London Pride makes a nice evergreen carpet in shady conditions with a haze of delicate little flowers in May. Red-leafed bugle, *Ajuga reptans atropurpurea* is low-growing and very thick. The dark lustrous foliage is evergreen and there are deep blue flowers in May. Also evergreen, or eversilver, but demanding sunshine and good drainage to be happy, is *Stachys lanata*, the woolly-leafed plant known as Lamb's Ears or Lamb's Lugs. The pale pink flowers are about 8in high and very pretty, though apt to be overlooked. Heathers will cover the ground in sunny spots but are such obviously moorland plants that they look out of place in a woodland setting. One very low evergreen plant which I believe will grow anywhere is *Sedum spurium* with rosettes of small rounded leaves and flat pink flower-heads on 4in stems. Every scrap of this will grow, on a path or a rubbish heap, on the soggy bank of a stream or sunbaked on a pile of rubble. I have never met a plant with such a will to live as this one.

Many rather rampant herbaceous plants could be used as ground-cover but are not really suitable in this setting. A 'blaze of colour' would be quite wrong. Mints of various kinds, lemon balm, thalictrum, hostas, and the striped grass called Gardener's Garters (*Phalaris arundinacea picta*) would fit in well as they have interesting leaves and the flowers are small or of subdued colouring. Most woodland flowers are pale, glimmering mysteriously in shaded places. The unusual plant Solomon's Seal has this quality, and pale yellow day-lilies will not look out of place. Foxgloves, especially the cream-coloured ones, are effective among trees and their foliage covers the ground all winter. They seed freely and perpetuate themselves—this year's seedlings will flower next year since they are biennial—but it is unwise to leave this too much to nature. Removal of the majority of the seeding spikes will limit the number of offspring but the plants may still need thinning. Another biennial, the Evening Primrose (*Oenethera biennis*), behaves in the same way and looks charming.

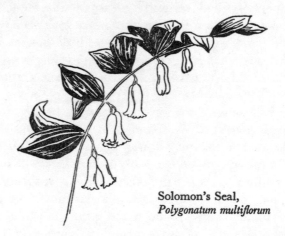

Solomon's Seal,
Polygonatum multiflorum

I have mentioned only common plants here, but many rare and splendid things could be grown if you have the means and the knowledge. The main thing about making a woodland garden is to clear the ground of the perennial weeds such as nettles, docks, ground elder and creeping buttercup, and to plant it at once before it becomes re-infested. Plot the positions of the trees first and put them in; then plant each yard of ground, as it becomes ready, with shrubs and ground-cover. A certain amount of hand weeding will be necessary at first but in a couple of years the work should be minimal. By their nature most ground-cover subjects are vigorous spreaders, but they must not be allowed to stifle developing shrubs. The majority of people find it more tedious to keep weeding areas of bare soil than to pull up and burn a few basketfuls of over exuberant carpeters twice a year. To get the right effect you need big drifts and bold masses, not one dainty shrub but three strong ones of the same kind, not half a dozen Rose of Sharon plants but thirty. That is why I name the common, prolific ones: you will often get them for nothing as they soon outgrow their allotted space in a conventional, well-disciplined garden, and people are glad to be rid of the surplus. One hefty clump of Rose of Sharon can be divided and each scrap of root planted about 12in apart to cover a considerable stretch of ground. These patches do need to be large—remember that they will become smaller as the shrubs grow larger—and they must run into each other to look natural. You do not want a symmetrical ring of foxgloves and then a patch of periwinkle; you want one to flow into the other, and a couple of foxgloves to occur in the periwinkles as if they had seeded there (and probably they will have done). Then too you must avoid balancing things, which seems to be a normal human instinct. The areas of ground-cover should *not* turn out to be roughly the same size; and if you have three rounded bushes at one side of the path, make sure you do not have rounded bushes of similar height at the opposite side. Choose instead something with a tall narrow shape and put an arching shrub or a prostrate conifer like *Juniperus pfitzeriana* beside it. A bold clump of bergenia can neighbour a very much larger expanse of something like woodruff or violets. Climbers can scramble up trees or sprawl on the ground as they prefer. Honeysuckle can be a killer because it winds right round the branches and trunk of its support, so it should be allowed to grow only on a mature tree, or a dead one. The various ornamental vines, *Clematis montana*, and ivies (which grow along, not around, trunks) are other possibilities. Where there is some sun the old Everlasting Pea, *Lathyrus latifolius*, will scramble over a stump or weave its way through shrubs such as *Cotoneaster horizontalis*. As well as the bright pink one, there is a white-flowered variety which is particularly pleasing.

I have talked about weed-smotherers, but some weeds may well be allowed a place in the woodland. Looked at without prejudice, many of them are very beautiful—consider cow-parsley, the wild purple mallow, and rosebay willow-herb. I let the wild arum or Jack-in-a-Pulpit grow in my garden under trees. The scarlet berries are poisonous but even a very small child could hardly mistake it for anything else, as it is such a peculiar plant. White dead-nettle is a very satisfying plant too, though if your mind automatically says 'weed' when you look at it, you will be blind to its charms. This came home to me when I admired a pretty pink trailer growing in an urn in a friend's garden and found that it was the pink convolvulus, bindweed, the scourge of my blackcurrant-bed. The large

Wild arum or
Jack-in-a-Pulpit

white convolvulus is really a splendid flower for those with eyes to see; so of course is the dandelion.

With some care, and an eye for effect, it is not difficult to create this sort of idealised woodland scene, which would make a fine setting for *A Midsummer Night's Dream*. Personal taste and imagination will suggest variations. Less common plants could be used, so that the blue haze under the trees turns out to be not bluebells but the heavenly blue poppy of the Himalayas, *Meconopsis betonicifolia*, which thrives in woodland conditions. Or a sunny woodland could be conjured up using a high proportion of golden-leafed or golden-green trees and shrubs.

Some people like 'odd' plants and some do not. I have read that the great gardener E. A. Bowles had a plant 'lunatic asylum' in his garden. One wonders how a plant qualified for admission. However, there are several plants which I regard as definitely peculiar, and any one of them would provide an unusual attraction in a woodland garden, and a talking point for visitors. I have even wondered what it would be like to plant them all together in junglelike profusion. Such a strange and exotic medley would look grotesque as background to a traditional country cottage, but if I ever lived in a very modern house with stark straight lines I should be tempted to surround it with all the curious and striking plants I could find.

What do I mean by odd? First, there are the peculiar trees with wildly twisted branches which provide such a weird silhouette in winter. One is a willow called *Salix matsudana tortuosa*; another the Corkscrew hazel, *Corylus avellana Contorta*. A monkey-puzzle tree has a bizarre appearance too, but it is only suitable for a large garden.

Next, there are those giant plants which look as if they have escaped from a jungle, like the huge rhubarb, *Rheum palmatum* with vast leaves, and flowers on 6ft stalks. As a matter of fact, ordinary culinary rhubarb growing in good damp soil attains a considerable size and is not to be despised for planting in a woodland garden. The leaves are splendid and large plume-like flowers often develop, though in the kitchen-garden they

would be removed on sight. Also rhubarb-like is *Gunnera
manicata* which in damp rich soil produces leaves 6–8ft across
and a prickly inflorescence. Quite different in appearance, the
giant hemlock, *Heracleum mantegazzianum*, has immense cow-
parsleylike heads, as big as umbrellas, on 8ft stalks. Then
there are the dramatic silver thistles: the one called *Onopordon
arabicum* reaches about 8ft in height and is less branchy than the
smaller *O. acanthium*, which has large heads of purplish flowers.
This name reminds me of *Acanthus spinosus*, the inspiration for
much sculptural decoration in Ancient Greece. It has huge,
deeply cut leaves and prickly spikes of purple flowers.

The Plume poppy, *Macleaya cordata*, carries its large inflorescences up to 8ft above the ground, with leaves all the
way up its stem. The huge lilac plume of *Eremurus robustus* is
about the same height, rising from a clump of grasslike foliage.
Then there is Pampas Grass, *Cortaderia argentea* and its rather
smaller variety, *Pumila*, which seldom exceeds 5ft tall. The
mental picture of its dusty plumes decorating Victorian dining-
rooms has obscured its exotic appearance. This is a plant to
put on a bank, so that its silvery heads catch the sunlight and
glitter against the sky. The yuccas are exotic too, in a different
way—reminiscent of deserts, somehow—with swordlike leaves
and impressive spikes of cream-coloured flowers. *Petasites
japonicus giganteus* has huge, rounded light green leaves and
makes impressive clumps. Then there are the yellow spires of
the mulleins or verbascums, *giganteum* and *bombyciferum*, up to
7ft tall; but most verbascums are biennials.

Only a large garden could accommodate the species rhododendrons, which are among the most extraordinary plants
which grow in Britain. They are the ancestors of the shrubs we
think of as rhododendrons today but they have an unearthly,
incredible quality as if they were survivals from the primeval
forests belonging to the dawn of history. In fact I suppose they
are if it is true, as I was once told, that they have remained
unchanged for 50 million years. *Rhododendron sino-grande* has
leaves 2–3ft long and 12in wide of a leathery substance, and

colossal creamy yellow flowers, while *R. macabeanum* and *R. falconeri* are equally imposing. I would love to try them though they grow well in only a few places. This is a dream akin to those of holidaymakers who look at the sub-tropical splendours of Tresco and imagine *Dasylirions* and *Cordyline australis* in their own back gardens.

If we cannot have these, we can probably manage that exotically named Chinese tree, *Ailanthus altissima*, the Tree of Heaven, which has arching, palmlike leaves about 5ft long. Another strange tree, though in a less obvious way, is *Ginkgo biloba*, sometimes called Maidenhair Tree because its leaves resemble those of the maidenhair fern on a larger scale. Though a conifer, its fan-shaped leaves turn a glorious yellow in autumn and fall off: it is not at all like any other conifer.

I could imagine the search for peculiar and exotic-looking plants becoming an obsession. As it is I am constantly coming across plants in public gardens and described in books which, though not so spectacular as some I have mentioned, have some quality of bold form and robust growth which would allow them to hold their own in such company. There is *Centaurea macrocephala*, the Great Golden Knapweed, growing 4–5ft high with a striking head of golden bloom; *Euphorbia wulfenii*, a spurge with great heads of lime-green flowers; *Fatsia japonica*, a shrub with big, glossy evergreen leaves and masses of white flowers in autumn; *Vitis coignetiae* whose huge vine leaves put on a spectacular colour display before they fall; even the globe artichokes and angelica from the kitchen-garden would not be out of place.

There would have to be no half-measures about this garden, nothing timid or dainty, and certainly no sundials or beds of floribundas. It would have to be planned in bold masses and strange silhouettes, deliberately theatrical. It could be organised to have as its focal point that uncompromising modern house we supposed at the start. If some garden feature were needed to end a vista or add point to a clearing, it would have to be something equally emphatic. Since Aztec gods in stone are not easy to find, I would suggest a massive, modern, abstract sculpture.

Chapter 4

Birdland

SOME KEEN gardeners would like to enclose their whole plot under a giant fruit-cage to keep out what they regard as feathered pests, but for most people birds add immeasurably to the sum of human pleasure just by existing. They certainly do more good than harm in a garden, and there is endless amusement and interest to be had from learning about them, and watching them, even on a bird-table. If they can be persuaded to take up residence, the whole fascinating process of nest-building, hatching and rearing can be seen, with luck. Birds provide companionship for lonely people. Budding naturalists can study wildlife on their own property and keen photographers have an unlimited source of rewarding subjects. Bored housewives are given an inducement to look outward rather than inward, and children can begin appreciating the other inhabitants of their native country at an impressionable age.

There is another consideration. As the demands of large-scale agricultural machinery do away annually with hundreds of miles of hedgerow, country lanes become hedgeless motor-ways, and our remaining woodlands dwindle, the natural habitat of many birds is lost. This is short-sighted from any point of view since birds are the best control for many insect pests. Lack of them means resorting to powerful insecticides with little-understood side effects such as poisons retained in foodstuffs and indiscriminate damage to other wildlife, in-

cluding the essential bee. Gardens can provide a valuable
alternative habitat for birds, and it is my experience that,
given a flourishing bird population, garden insecticides are
seldom needed.

How can birds be lured into a garden; and what kind do
they favour? Anyone who has ever bought an old house which
has been empty for some time will know the answer to the
second question. Neglected. One thinks of Victorian rectories,
long vacant because of their size and inconvenience, with an
acre or so of abandoned grounds, thick with the shrubberies
which were fashionable in their day. These are invariably alive
with birds. Dense evergreen plantings offer sheltered roosting-
and nesting-places. Thistles and other weeds running riot in
uncut grass provide seeds, while ancient apple trees, blackberry
brambles, wild raspberry, unclipped privet and ivy spread a
feast of fruit and berry. This kind of garden may not be
attractive as a garden but it is a haven for birds and other
wildlife such as hedgehogs, dormice and badgers.

I am not going to suggest reproducing such a tangled
wilderness in the average garden. Even when tended, Victorian
shrubberies were depressing, with their limited range of evergreens used in sombre masses. They were often too close to the
house, darkening the windows and giving the children night-
mares. The dwelling itself was probably smothered in ivy and
looked as if it were drowning in foliage—which, after a few
years' neglect, it frequently did! However, the twisted stems
and sheltering leaves of ivy offer a safe home for many birds,
as do the dense firs and tangled laurels. We can learn from
this, though aiming at a different effect.

A garden will be popular with birds if it is relatively undisturbed. One which is intensively cultivated in all its corners,
with clipped hedges and shrubs kept to exact dimensions, will
harbour few wild things. The bird-lover's ideal garden will
provide the maximum enjoyment for the minimum of upkeep.
In previous chapters we have looked at gardens which need
little maintenance, and birds will find them attractive; but we

can carry this a stage further and try to cater for the birds'
special needs. This does not rule out cultivated ground, of
course. You could have a rose-garden (which the tits will keep
free of aphids). You can have a kitchen-garden, and the local
robin and several thrushes and blackbirds will gather round to
eat the insects turned up as you dig it. You can have a border
of perennials, a rockery, a pool, or anything else, but if there
are no suitable nesting-places you will have only visiting birds,
not residents.

The birds' primary need is safety. If you have a cat, or mean
to get one, it is unfair to encourage birds. They will become
tame, even hand-tame if you have enough patience, and
consequently careless. To introduce a kitten at that stage is a
betrayal of trust. Visiting cats cannot be kept out so careful
consideration must be given to the placing of bird-tables, baths
and nest-boxes. Dogs are seldom a hazard to birds, and often
protect them by keeping cats away.

Thousands of people encourage birds by throwing crusts on
to the lawn, but a proper bird-table would be more enjoyable
from both points of view. These can be bought, but a simple
one is best and very easy to make. First consider where to put
it. Some people put a bird-table at the far end of the garden
where nobody can see the visitors, if indeed anyone remembers
to put out food. It will be most patronised in winter, so the best
position is about 6ft away from a kitchen or sitting-room
window. Here it will be easy to watch, less vulnerable to attack
by predators, and less easily forgotten. Where an elderly or
handicapped person is much confined to one room, a bird-table
provides amusement and company. If this is an upstairs room
a table can be attached to an outside sill, if the window is not
too high, and replenished from inside. If the height of the sill,
or the fact that a person must lie in bed makes this impracti-
cable, a bracket can be screwed to the top of the window-frame
and a bird-feeder or a lump of suet on a string can be suspended
from it. Many small birds will come visiting.

Incidentally, encouraging birds to come to a bird-table does impose a moral obligation to keep it supplied, especially in severe weather when the need is greatest. The density of birds in established suburban gardens is far greater than in any kind of natural woodland, and this puts a great strain on available food supplies.

A simple bird-table is easy to make. The top should be at least 15in square—one blackbird can take up a surprising amount of room. It can be rectangular, or even round, but a little roof is not an asset unless seagulls are a nuisance. Birds do not mind getting wet but many are afraid to go in under a roof. Also it prevents their being seen properly. A rim round the edge is an aid to perching and prevents the food from being scattered in scuffles, but the corners should be left open, or holes drilled in the base, for drainage. About 5ft of post above ground and 18in below is about right. Cup-hooks screwed under the bottom allow lumps of suet, nut feeders, half-coconuts and meaty bones to be suspended.

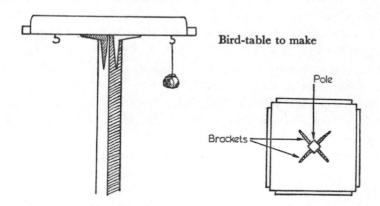

Bird-table to make

Pole

Brackets

To ensure the birds' safety, there should be no handy fence or overhanging branch from which a predator could reach the table, or thick bushes or tall plants nearby which would give a prowler cover. Some birds prefer to hop around the base of the bird-table. The shy little accentor or dunnock (also called the hedge-sparrow, though it is not a sparrow) picks up what other

birds knock down, and chaffinches also often feed off the ground.
Grass or a low ground-covering plant is best for 8–9ft around
the post. A patch of grass will be regularly worked over by
blackbirds and thrushes in search of worms, and starlings
dealing with leather-jackets and other pests.

If you are not knowledgeable about birds, a small manual
like *The Observer's Book of Birds* will help identification. Keep
it on the nearest window-sill. Among your visitors you may
expect to see robins, sparrows, dunnocks, thrushes, nuthatches,
blackbirds and two or three kinds of finch. Suet and nuts
attract several varieties of tit as well as greenfinches. The
colourful little goldfinch never comes to my bird-table, though
groups feed on the weed seeds in my orchard during the
summer. I have seen a wren on the suet—he comes sideways
up the post as tits often do—but this is uncommon. These tiny
insect-eaters are reluctant to accept bird-table food, and this is
one reason why so many die in hard winters.

In winter, especially in bad weather, you may have an
unexpected visitor such as a redwing or fieldfare separated
from the flock or, if there are woods or parks nearby, jays,
pigeons, crossbills or woodpeckers. A squirrel, too, may become
a regular caller on sunny days. A solitary moorhen once spent
a whole February in my garden, industriously searching the
compost pit for worms, and for a couple of days a lapwing
stalked about the orchard before flying off to join the flock on
the open fields.

Magpies seldom visit a bird-table, especially if it is close to
the house, but starlings sometimes come in a crowd and clear
the table in minutes. It is difficult to discourage them without
scaring away other birds. Some people put out big chunks of
bread for the starlings first, hoping that they will fly away
when it is eaten so that more delectable bits can be put out for
the others; but I do not think they are so easily duped. They
are among the most successful of birds, being intelligent,
greedy, omnivorous and adaptable. Though pushing, they are
not aggressive to other birds. Excellent mimics, they are often

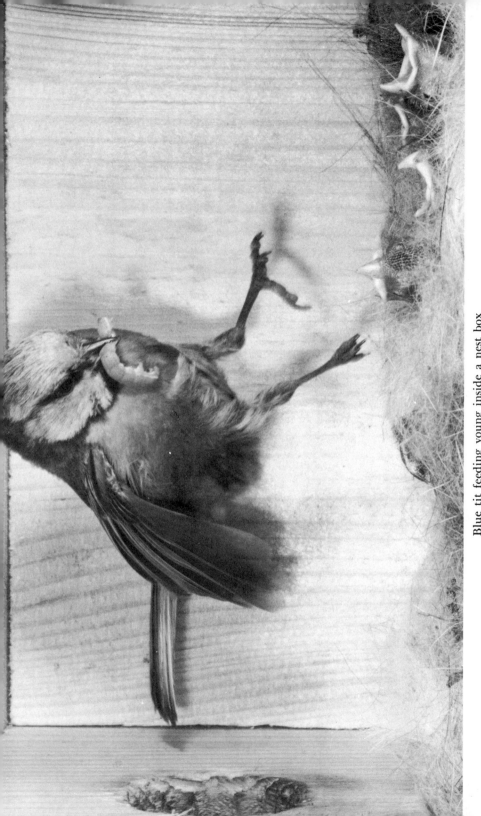

Blue tit feeding young inside a nest box

Daffodils (*Narcissi*) naturalized under fruit trees

highly amusing as well as useful, so it may be as well to put up with their less pleasing traits.

Bread is usually offered as food. Wholemeal is better than white. Put all crusts and crumbs into a bowl in the kitchen and pour on some hot water. Soaked bread is better for birds; also it does not blow off the table and is less likely to be carried away in large pieces. Cake, cereals, cheese, fish and meat scraps, raisins and currants, bacon rinds and all sorts of nuts are relished. Tits like coconuts, but do not leave these hanging in spring because nestlings cannot digest the flesh. Never offer desiccated coconut which can be fatal even to adults. Blackbirds particularly relish squashy or even rotten apples. Mealworms are enjoyed by some birds, but many people cannot bear to feed these beetle larvae live to birds. Robins will sometimes come to the hand for them, but they should be given sparingly. We had a robin who learnt to balance, flapping wildly, on the suet-lumps and help himself, but he never became neat and agile like the tits. Starlings will also attempt to do this and will often break the string, so tie the suet up close to the table to give the greenfinches and titmice a better chance. One warning about suet: when most of the fat has been eaten, the remaining stringy mesh of tissue should be taken down. It has been known for a tomtit to get his claws so entangled in this that he was found in the early morning still suspended and dead from exhaustion and exposure. Some people make 'bird cake', which is a mixture of porridge oats, scraps, currants, crumbs and whatever is available moulded together with melted fat and allowed to cool. Lumps can be stuck in the crevices of tree bark to tempt small birds which are too shy to come to the table. Wild-bird seed in packets has sometimes meant the difference between life and death to seed-eaters during snowy spells. It is better to put out a little each day rather than half a packet one day and nothing more for a week.

Birds will also come for water, especially in a built-up area where standing water is scarce. A shallow pool they can walk

D

into is best. Birds bathe in both winter and summer, and starlings especially will splash about merrily if the ice is broken on their bath. Never be tempted to add glycerine to the water to prevent it from freezing, because this is harmful. The water needs to be only about 2in deep. Where there is a little stream or natural rill, the bank might be dug out to provide a 'bathing beach' away from the main current, but make sure that there is no cover for cats to creep up on the 'bathers'.

Bird-tables and water supplies will bring birds to the garden, but the garden itself determines whether any will take up residence and raise families there. Two main considerations are housing and natural food supplies. Usually a desirable nest-site involves a tree, bush or creeper, but some birds adopt strange places to build in and in general these are the ones which will use a well-placed nesting-box. Everyone has heard of tits which have nested in a letter-box. I have known them build a nest in a hollow garden gnome whose arm had broken off leaving a neat round hole. Robins will use an old saucepan or kettle lodged in a hedge, or in my case an open biscuit tin full of seed packets on a greenhouse shelf. They, and sparrows, are the easiest to fix up with artificial sites. Some species are difficult. Swifts nest in holes under eaves, where they cannot be seen. Housemartins stick their nests on walls just below the eaves and choose houses by their own mysterious selection system. There are artificial nests which might persuade them to come, but sparrows usually occupy them first. Like swallows, martins must have mud available from a local river or pond for nest-building. Swallows often build in more accessible places such as a beam in a garage or tool-shed: if this happens, a door or window must be left open until the nestlings fly. The majority of birds seen in our gardens nest in a fork of a tree or shrub using twigs, grass, roots, moss, feathers, hair, wool, even paper and string. A starling's nest I saw recently had a piece of polythene neatly incorporated: a modern couple there!

Do not think of cutting down any established tree in the garden: even a dead one, covered with creeper, is an asset.

Russian vine (*Polygonum baldschuanicum*) is a fast-growing climber with pretty, foamlike sprays of white flowers. It is rampant and suitable only for a tall tree, a hedge grown thin and straggly, or a large outhouse. *Clematis montana*, pink-flowered or white, also climbs quickly but is less overwhelming. The self-clinging Virginia creeper (*Parthenocissus quinquefolia*) is suitable, and so is the decorative *Vitis coignetiae*. These are deciduous, so they will not give winter cover. Ivy will. Common ivy is a really beautiful plant, but familiarity has tended to blunt our appreciation of it. About 5ft up it changes the nature of its leaves and produces heads of strangely attractive greenish flowers, followed by black berries. I have seen the stump of a dead cedar covered entirely with ivy so that it made a symmetrical, round-headed 'tree' some 15ft high. It was always known as 'the Ivy Tree'. Inside it was a fantastic mass of birds' nests, and the heaped up dust-dry materials of what looked like a century's accumulation of disintegrating ones, slowly sifting down among the twisted stems. The stump had crumbled in places and other nests lurked in the hollows and crevices. The 'tree' might have been even more fascinating if a coloured ivy had been used. There is *Hedera canariensis Variegata*, also known as Gloire de Marengo, and the variegated form of the Persian ivy, *Hedera colchica*; a golden form of the common ivy, *Hedera helix*, called *Buttercup*; and a silver-edged one called *Marginata* or *Silver Queen*. *Hedera hibernica* is a green ivy with large bright leaves. Some of the most ornamental ivies grow very slowly, so make sure about this. An alternative is evergreen honeysuckle, *Lonicera japonica*, which soon shoots up and has creamy flowers.

Starlings seem addicted to nesting in creepers on walls. I have seen them in *Clematis montana* growing profusely over a garage, and in a far less luxuriant growth of the large purple-flowered *C. jackmanii* in the angle of a garden wall. On the whole, birds avoid climbers on small dwellings, perhaps because these are apt to be more trimmed and trained than elsewhere. On a larger house, well-established ivy or Virginia creeper or wistaria will probably be used, and this is often a

good place to put a robin's nest-box or some other container
which might be adopted.

Only established trees make acceptable nest-sites, so cherish
any you have. Laburnums and ornamental cherries are seldom
favoured, but I have often seen nests in Lawson's cypress which
can easily grow 10ft tall in five years. These are often planted
as a screen along a boundary but they also make good specimen
trees or groups. The beautiful coloured kinds unfortunately
take much longer to reach a useful size. Such evergreens also
provide sheltered roosting-places for birds in winter.

Apart from trees and creepers, strong hedges and large
shrubs provide adequate nesting-sites. Even a clipped hedge of
beech or laurel, for instance, will sometimes contain a nest or
two. If this happens, leave a section of hedge unclipped until
the nestlings fly. As a very rough guide, most songbirds incubate
their eggs for about two weeks, and the young birds will fly in
another two. However, the sort of unclipped hedge or belt of
shrubs and small trees described in previous chapters offers the
best natural nesting-sites in a garden. In the eighteenth century
when the commons were enclosed, thousands of miles of 'quick-
set' or hawthorns were planted as boundaries and windbreaks
on farmland, and are now disappearing just as rapidly in the
name of efficiency. Nothing suits birds better than high spiky
hawthorns, full of forked twigs that are admirable for nest-sites.
Thrushes and dunnocks, wrens, blackbirds and warblers,
greenfinches and chaffinches, and even magpies, have used
mine. Equally popular is a mixed hedge of oak and holly, elm
and elder, hawthorn, hornbeam and much else. One holly,
unclipped except when some is cut at Christmas, has in my
garden sheltered a pair of blackbirds every spring for nine
years, though it is unlikely that it is the same pair. A hedge
such as this will need more control in a garden than it would
between fields, but the work consists mainly of removing
awkwardly shaped branches, or the top of something threaten-
ing to grow huge. A gorse thicket often contains nests and is
proof against most kinds of interference. It is not a plant for a

small garden, but where there is space it will grow in poor soil or on a dry windswept bank where nothing else will thrive. A seldom pruned flowering shrub like forsythia, lilac or *Buddleia globosa* is often chosen for nesting. It is amazing how well-anchored are these flimsy little homes. During one winter I noticed a nest which was exposed when the leaves dropped from a lilac bush, and though gales blew the top rail off a nearby wooden archway and uprooted a laburnum, the nest was still securely in place when the buds began to break again.

Where nesting-places are few, nest-boxes can be put up. Most of the boxes on sale are decorative rather than practical, and are apt to prove disappointing. They are usually too small inside, especially as regards depth. A neat little perch under the hole in a tit-box offers a foothold to magpie, grey squirrel, weasel or other predator and is not a good idea. The illustration shows two versions of an easily made box (p. 60). The one with the hole will be used by tits, tree-sparrows and nuthatches. The hole should be $1\frac{1}{8}$in diameter for tits, $1\frac{1}{4}$in for tree-sparrows, and between $1\frac{1}{8}$in and $1\frac{1}{2}$in for nuthatches which will reduce it with mud if they think it is too big. House sparrows will take over a box with a $1\frac{1}{2}$in hole, and are quite capable of enlarging a smaller one to suit themselves. The open-fronted style is preferred by robins, spotted flycatchers and pied wagtails, but it is very vulnerable and should be carefully sited.

Boxes should be fastened to the north or north-east side of a wall or tree-trunk if the young birds are not to be overheated. Never put one where the sun's rays will fall directly on it. Height is not especially important as long as there is no easy access for a predator. High boxes are safer from cats but more likely to be investigated by squirrels. If there are no human predators about, 5ft up a blank wall might be safe, whereas 12ft might be necessary elsewhere. A box on an isolated bare pole is quite popular, but it must be sheltered from sun and driving rain. The edges of woods, or the trees around a glade or open space are generally preferred to the centres of woods by birds building nests, so take this preference into account

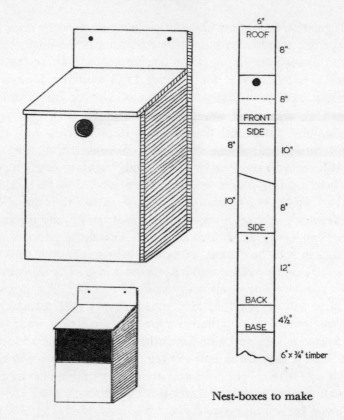

Nest-boxes to make

when putting up boxes. Trees and shrubs surrounding a lawn or pond reproduce similar conditions. There should be a clear flight-path to the box. Tits begin prospecting for sites very early, so put their boxes up during February. Mid-March will be soon enough for other birds. When fixing a nest-box to a tree, tilt it slightly forward to stop rain from driving into the entrance, either by choosing a slightly sloping branch or trunk and attaching the box to the lower side of it, or by using a wedge on a vertical surface. The birds will build their nest level inside.

There is no need to put any nest materials in the box, but if you leave out a collection of bits of cotton and cottonwool, pillow feathers, animal hair, scraps of string and so on, perhaps hung in a mesh bag on the bird-table or spread on the grass, you may find it amusing to watch the birds helping themselves. I once inspected several sparrow nests built under the eaves and found many pieces of brightly coloured embroidery wool, chocolate-wrappers, a postage stamp and a strip of 'caps' from a toy pistol, as well as sprigs of arabis and forget-me-nots, among the building materials in use.

Pretty, 'rustic' nest-boxes made from bark-covered logs can be bought, but these are usually too small inside. A log 9–10in in diameter and 10–12in long would be needed to provide adequate space. Where the entrance hole of a nest-box is less than 6in above the base, the upstretched heads of the nestlings may be seen and grasped by a predator. The lid of a rustic box must fit tightly so that it does not leak and cannot be pushed off. The top usually pushes in like the lid of a paint tin but when it gets wet and swells it often splits, or the log does. A round lid nailed or screwed on top is better. In practice, it is easier to split the log and hollow each half separately before reassembling it with glue and pins. This sort of nest-box can be hung on a wire handle against the trunk of a tree, in a suitable place where it will not be violently shaken by winds. The handle should be secured to the hook so that it cannot be accidentally knocked off.

On an ivy-covered wall, a flowerpot fastened to a stout stem and sheltered by leaves may be adopted by robins. Tins, coconut shells or other containers may be tried, but they should have drainage holes drilled in the bottom to prevent flooding. If a wall can be used which is at right angles to another with a window in it, an excellent observation point is provided.

Once a nest-box is occupied it should be left alone. Often there are doors and roofs which open to allow the young to be examined, but in the case of amateurs this usually results in the parent birds deserting. I prefer roofs to be screwed on so that they are more weatherproof but can be removed for cleaning. Hardwoods are the most durable but the roofs of softwood boxes can be covered with roofing-felt for longer life. Cedar is light, lasts well, and weathers attractively. Birds do not object to preservatives, even creosote, and these do make boxes less conspicuous. The use of a preservative is probably advisable on softwood boxes, particularly on the backs which catch the water running down the trunk. The grain of the wood should run vertically down the sides and down the roof to help water drain off. Wood ¾in thick is best for durability and insulation. It need not be planed.

Lastly, there is the question of natural food supplies. In any garden there are enough insects to provide a comfortable existence for many feathered carnivores, if insecticides are not used. Obviously if a garden is made sterile with poisonous sprays, powders and pellets there will be no food for insect-eaters like wrens, robins and thrushes or, incidentally, for shrews, hedgehogs and slow-worms. Some people assume that all insects are harmful, but many are useful and even necessary. Slugs, snails, aphids and caterpillars can wreak havoc in a kitchen-garden but these are precisely the ones which birds will keep in check, given the chance. It is on record that a family of tits consumed some 18,000 caterpillars in three weeks. Few modern houses offer suitable conditions for nesting swifts, but a pair feeding young may easily catch 20,000 flying insects and small spiders *every day*. A bird's metabolism requires huge quantities of food, relative to its weight, to maintain its rapid development, and the parents too must eat well to keep up such an output of energy. Some birds which are normally seed-eaters, like house sparrows, feed their nestlings on insects, presumably because of the higher protein content. I used to leave suet on the bird-table all summer in case the tits found themselves hard-pressed, but they never came for it, so they must have found sufficient natural food—which is better for them, and the garden. I do go on putting out bread and scraps in small amounts, so that we can enjoy the sight of family parties. Starlings, thrushes and chaffinches bring their large fluffy chicks, which squat with gaping beaks waiting for their overworked parents to cram food into them. This does no harm as a supplement to more nourishing natural food.

Seed-eaters enjoy a wide range of seeds and berries. There will be some weed seeds available if your grass is rough, but do not be in too great a hurry to cut off dead flowers in autumn. Seeds of Michaelmas daisies, *Buddleia davidii*, cornflowers, sunflowers and teasels will be enjoyed.

Fruit-eaters will eat cultivated fruits, of course. I gave up growing redcurrants because I was left with none, but I do grow raspberries, gooseberries and blackcurrants without protection and without noticeable loss. The secret is to provide a wide range of alternative fruits for the birds, if you want to grow some for yourself and still encourage birdlife in the garden.

Many of the shrubs and trees which provide nesting-places also bear useful berries. Hawthorn is one, though the double-flowered varieties do not fruit. Holly must be female to produce berries and must have a male tree somewhere near. The naming of the variegated kinds causes confusion, because *Golden King* is a female and bears berries while the male *Golden Queen* does not. White-margined *Silver Queen* is also male. Some nurserymen can be vague about this so make sure what you are getting. Free-berrying green forms include *Pyramidalis*, and the hermaphrodite *Polycarpa* which needs no pollinator. Perry's Silver Weeping holly, *Madame Briot*, and *Handsworth Silver* are other variegated hollies which usually bear well. Provision of a male tree is often enough to bring a reluctant female into fruit.

The elder will grow anywhere and produces plentiful fruit. The brilliant red berries of the rowan are a favourite food of the wax-wing which comes from northern Europe in considerable numbers some years, around September. The wax-wings are often too late for the rowans because thrushes and blackbirds like them too. The whitebeam is related to the rowan, has silver-backed leaves and crimson berries, and deserves a good position in the garden. Blackbirds find the berries of *Cotoneaster horizontalis* irresistible. This grows 1½ft tall, except against a wall where it arches up to 6ft, continually spreading sideways. Other berry-bearing cotoneasters range from prostrate forms such as *C. dammeri* and *C. conspicuus decorus* to small trees like *C. frigidus* and the evergreen *C. watereri*. *Cotoneaster simonsii* is sometimes used as hedging up to about 6ft high. Pyracantha berries will be eaten and also the plump, translucent crimson fruit of guelder rose (*Viburnum opulus*).

The squashy cylindrical fruit of the hardy fuchsia is avidly eaten by birds. Even where it is cut to the ground in winter it will spring up to about 4ft during the following summer. In favoured districts *Fuchsia magellanica Riccartonii* will make a 6ft hedge or small tree. Unclipped privet produces handsome black berries, and crab-apples are another source of food. Less common, but only for milder districts, is *Arbutus unedo*, the Strawberry Tree, which grows wild in south-west Ireland. It is evergreen and may grow to 20ft tall, with white pitcher-shaped flowers followed by round knobby fruit which does not really resemble a strawberry in appearance. The fruit tastes very insipid to us but birds relish it.

Modern gardens can seldom accommodate an oak or a beech of fruit-bearing size, a pine tree, or a hornbeam whose winged nuts are enjoyed by hawfinches. Numerous chaffinches come to feast on the seeds from a large pine outside my gate whenever the wind brings down the cones. Hazel or cobnuts are a practical proposition and the catkins look pretty in February. These are *Corylus*. Many kinds of wild plum such as sloe and bullace can be grown in a hedgerow, and also the Myrobalan or cherry plum (*Prunus cerasifera*). *Prunus cistena* is a smaller relative with red leaves and black/purple fruits. Birds are supposed to prefer the black fruits of *P. padus*, the Bird Cherry, to the cultivated sort. The wild cherry, the gean or mazzard, *Prunus avium*, is bigger than most cherry trees. It has edible fruit and splendid autumn colouring. The beautiful double-flowered kind does not bear fruit. Laurels, growing naturally, produce berries and so does the so-called 'spotted laurel', *Aucuba japonica Maculata*, but this is female and the green male form nearby is necessary to ensure berries. There is a variegated male form called *Picturata*, but it is not common.

The barberry, *Berberis vulgaris*, with edible fruit, is deciduous and colours well in autumn. It has a purple-leafed variety. *B. thunbergii* has scarlet berries and grows to about 4ft: its red-leafed form is taller. *B. wilsonae* is about 2ft tall but spreading, with clusters of coral fruit. *B. darwinii* is the best known of the evergreen varieties, growing about 8ft tall with tiny holly-like leaves, orange flowers and blue, bloomy berries. *B. stenophylla* is also evergreen and *B. irwinii* is similar but much smaller. There are dozens more in this extensive family. Mahonias, until recently, were included with berberis. The commonest is *Mahonia aquifolium*, once called Oregon grape, with blue-black berries. The creeping *M. repens rotundifolia* grows 2–3ft tall with spineless leaves, yellow plumes of flowers and black, bloomy berries.

The common Spindle Tree, *Euonymus europaea*, has pretty, rose-coloured fruits with bright orange seeds, which are poisonous to children but not to birds. This applies also to the scarlet berries of *Daphne mezereum*, which are avidly snapped up by finches before they are really ripe. This little bush bears its strongly scented, purply pink flowers in February and is an

Ivy berries which ripen in early spring

asset in any garden. Finally, the black berries of the ivy, which ripen during the winter, prove a boon to thrushes and blackbirds in March and April when all other supplies are exhausted.

If a garden is planned primarily for birds it should have a simple layout which will not require much work to keep it looking attractive. A grassy glade surrounded by trees and shrubs, or a broad pathway with planting at both sides, is probably the easiest arrangement for a small garden, and it allows for endless personal variation in the juxtaposition of colour, shrub form, leaf type and so on. A country's wildlife is dependent on that country's own plants and the insects associated with them, so the best plants for the birds will tend to be the cheap and easily obtainable native ones. If these form the backbone of the plant material, there is no reason why some exotic shrubs or unusual specimen trees cannot be included to make a striking accent or to complete a picture. The main thing is to study each shrub's requirements as to sun, shade, space and soil, give it a good start and then as far as possible leave it alone. The garden will improve every year and become easier to maintain, and the birds will soon show their approval.

Chapter 5

The Plot in Front

THE FRONT GARDEN problem is a recent pheno-
menon. If you look at the illustrations in any pre-war
book on gardens it is noticeable that only in very large
plots was any provision made for the motor-car. People who
lived in small houses with small gardens did not own cars.
Books published in the 1930s illustrate substantial double-
fronted villas and architect-designed houses on half-acre plots
with no more than a small gate at the roadside and a straight
path to the front door. A few are shown with garages and gates
opening on to a side or back road. Where there was a drive
leading to the front door, it occupied a small proportion of the
available ground and was easily absorbed into a scheme of
wide lawns and lavish planting, with the garage concealed
behind shrubs.

Things are different today. The typical modern plot is
narrow and divided into two separate areas by the house and
garage, but the owner will probably have a car, possibly two,
which must be accommodated in the tiny front garden. The
drive-in to the garage, and probably a turning space too, will
take up a large proportion of the available ground. The problem is how to incorporate so much hard surface into a scheme
which is pleasant-looking, not too demanding, suits the house,
and at the same time has something distinctive about it. It is
harder still to find a satisfactory answer if you feel strongly that
front gardens should contain lawns and flower-beds.

Since the front garden is primarily an access area for you, your visitors and tradesmen, it is as well to come to terms with this factor at once and to stop hankering after the front gardens of yesteryear. In the past, builders tended to provide a broad strip of concrete connecting the road and garage, with a narrow branch or sometimes a separate small path to the front door. More recently a three-point turning space within the garden has been thought desirable to avoid backing out on to the road. If the garage is set back beyond the house, a wide strip along the house-front will form a T-junction for turning; but where house and garage are in line, the usual system is a sort of cul-de-sac jutting into the remaining piece of ground. This may be practical, but it imposes a stark pattern which is difficult to absorb into an attractive garden plan. If the end of the cul-de-sac were curved into a semicircle, it would be a good place for a piece of sculpture or a shallow concrete bowl planted with flowers: this would give it some visual point and satisfy the eye.

Incorporating this T-turning into a larger area of paving is another way of 'losing' it. As it will not be driven over, the ground between it and the front of the house could have suitable trailing and dwarf plants between the paving slabs, or it could be furnished with a seat, and tubs containing flowers or shrubs. It might be raised a step or two above the rest. The remaining corner might then be planted with a specimen tree and grass, or with a mass of shrubs to give more privacy.

Where the frontage is wide enough, a semicircular drive with two gateways, like the carriage drive of a Victorian house, is still an efficient form of access, and it leaves space for shrubs to screen the house. A turning circle, needing only one gateway, is also practical where there is room, but it would have to be 35–40ft across. Carried out in concrete or tarmac it might look rather like a petrol-station forecourt. Gravel needs regular raking and rolling unless it is tar-sprayed and surfaced, but with shrubs at its edge it could look dignified and uncluttered. It might also have a grass plat or bed of low shrubs in the centre. A really modern house might look well with its whole front area gravelled and the visual interest provided by strongly shaped shrubs in concrete pots—grouped, not standing about like sentries—and a belt of roadside shrubs for privacy.

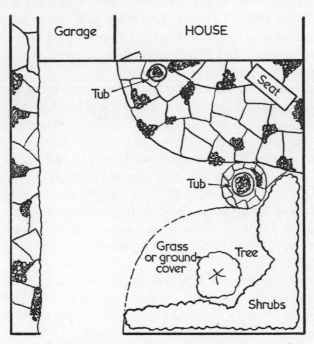

Disguising the concrete turning space

Plain concrete in quantity is not easy to live with, but it can be coloured to a more sympathetic tone at the mixing stage. Paving slabs are of many colours and textures, but all paving on which cars will stand should be bedded in a 2in concrete base. Part of the attraction of natural-stone crazy paving is its uneven surface, but the pressure from wheeled traffic is apt to tilt the stones and crack the mortar. A 'crazy' effect can be obtained (more cheaply too) with broken concrete slabs which have a flat surface if they are properly laid. Do make sure you really want crazy paving: it does not look right everywhere and could turn out to be an expensive mistake. Concrete slabs are available in green and tan and a mustardy yellow, grey and red and black, but think twice before mixing them together. I have seen a front garden with multi-coloured crazy paving, further enlivened with a mass of African marigolds and a garage-door painted purple. The result was not a happy one though it was certainly distinctive! A restrained scheme does not pall quickly, and plants, perhaps in painted wooden tubs or troughs, can be used to add colour.

Whatever hard surface is chosen for it, do make sure that your driveway is wide enough. You should be able to open the car doors and step out in comfort, *not* into a flower-bed. You should be able to get past to put a pushchair in the boot without scratching the bodywork. If you intend to wash the car yourself, decide where and plan accordingly. You should be able to get right round it. Remember too that few plants benefit from foliar feeding with detergents! An existing driveway can be widened with a border of paving slabs or bricks on one or both sides. This often improves the effect of plain concrete.

Still facing up to the demands of the car, ask yourself if you want gates. Are you likely to open and close them each time you go in or out? Probably only about two car-owners in twenty ever shut their gates. Many have never fitted any. Others have removed them after they were damaged or fell to pieces and never replaced them. The objection to open gateways is that other people use them for turning and parking their cars. Against this must be balanced the bother of opening and shutting them for yourself, and shutting them after the postman, the milkman, the paperboy ... as well as painting, oiling and mending them. It is usually a simple matter to put a gate between the front and back gardens to ensure that children or dogs are safely confined, leaving the front open for easy access.

Whether you decide to have gates or not, it is a good idea to set the entrance about 6ft back from the boundary and to

A cottage garden path

(*left*) Cream-splashed periwinkles make cheerful ground cover

(*right*) Elephant's Ears, *Bergenia*, forms solid evergreen cover

splay the hedge or fence to give better visibility. An occasional car may turn in it but the advantages should outweigh this. Hedging or shrubs close to a gateway should not exceed 4ft in height: 3ft is better. A pinched entrance, besides being difficult to negotiate, is anything but an inviting approach to a house.

If you do not want gates, do you want a fence, hedge or wall? Privacy can be achieved by other means, and the fence or hedge which is high enough to prevent people from looking over may also cut out a lot of light and make the front garden a gloomy little plot. If you do want a permanent barrier, try to relate it to the style of the house and what you plan for the rest of the front garden. For modern houses, the imaginative use of openwork concrete blocks is rewarding. Honeysuckle, clematis, and various vines including *Vitis coignetiae* and the purple, green and white variegated *Parthenocissus henryana*, will climb over and through such a wall in a most attractive way. Sometimes a front garden is a sunny spot where, given privacy, it would be pleasant to sit. These concrete blocks or strong, square wooden trellis with climbers could be used on the side boundary, roadside, and part way along the drive to enclose a paved courtyard, without the boxlike effect which a more solid fencing would give. Some seating and containers of flowers would make a pleasant little outdoor 'room' of this often wasted space.

If there is no fence, people will stray on to the grass or whatever you plant, so some way of marking the boundary is generally desirable. One possibility is to build up the ground a little inside the boundary and have a low brick or stone-faced bank. Low retaining walls of proper brickwork look neat, but they tempt children to walk along the top. The raised level also prevents sweet-papers and crisp-packets from blowing in off the pavement. A stone curb might be used to define the boundary, with shrubs planted behind it. If spiny shrubs like pyracantha, dwarf Japanese quince and berberis varieties are put at the roadside, they might well escape damage.

Having provided room for the car and good visibility, we are

E

probably left with a squarish or quadrant-shaped piece of ground inside the front boundary and possibly a narrow strip running down the side boundary to the garage. Side boundaries are often a cause of dispute. If a hedge is planted you must hope that your neighbour will trim the other side of it or let you go round and do it. Hedges often take up more room than was anticipated unless they are very well maintained. Neighbours might benefit from getting together on the question of mutual boundaries. A strong trellis on which both sides could grow climbers would certainly look prettier and should give more pleasure than a barricade of creosoted boards.

This narrow strip beside the drive may be only 12–18in wide. It is not a good place for roses or wall-shrubs with thorns, which will do neither the car's cellulose nor people getting out on that side any good. Choose a tough but soft-leafed climber such as *Clematis montana*, one of the ornamental vines already mentioned, or *Vitis vinifera Brandt* which has edible fruit (given a southern aspect and a good summer). Honeysuckle—perhaps the evergreen one—or a silver or gold variegated ivy are alternatives. Suitable wall-shrubs like *Ceanothus* and winter-sweet (*Chimonanthus fragrans*) could also be used.

Man-holes are often a feature of front gardens, and the smaller the plot the more obvious they are. They often seem to be set in the most awkward places and at the oddest angles, but in many cases they can be successfully hidden from view or at least made less obtrusive. Covers with a shallow rim can be obtained: these can be filled with concrete, tarmac or gravel to blend with path or drive. If the man-hole occurs where there is to be a shrub or flower-bed, it can be easily concealed. Bushy shrubs planted at the side will spread their branches over it. *Cotoneaster horizontalis* spreads sideways and is often recommended for this purpose, but I would prefer one of the prostrate junipers such as *Juniperus pfitzeriana Aurea* or *J. sabina tamariscifolia* which are evergreen. In a bed of perennials, billowing plants like gypsophila or catmint will spread themselves over a man-hole, and so will trailers such as arabis if near the front of the bed. A man-hole in what was planned to be an unbroken expanse of grass is a more difficult problem. If it is near the middle, one of the fibreglass troughs which are made to fit could be filled with plants and placed on top; or a stone slab could cover the iron lid and act as a base for a piece of sculpture or an urn. The slab must not be cemented in place, as the lid has to be accessible for lifting in case of need. The worst problem is when the intrusive lid comes near the edge of the proposed grass plot. It is then best to adapt your plan to include the lid in either the flower-bed or the paving, whichever adjoins the grass. A bold curve taking in the man-hole will look most natural, but if this should not be possible and a rather obvious recess results, it can be made to look intentional by putting a striking plant there, or a bird-bath or ornament if it is a hard surface.

If the levels are right, it is possible to pave over the top of the man-hole, providing the slabs are bedded in sand and a tool can be inserted between to lift them if necessary. If the man-hole stands up too high already this may not be possible, though surrounding slabs can probably be laid flush with it to make it less obtrusive. A concrete-filled lid will blend quite well with random rectangular paving, so long as the man-hole is not at an angle: it might even be worth laying the slabs diagonally if that is the case. The problem is different in every garden but is seldom insoluble. At the least the rusty lid can be given a coat of tar or cement paint according to its surrounding hard surface. It will wear off, but it is not a great chore to renew it.

What to do with the remaining ground? Something which must be taken into account is the sad increase in pointless vandalism. In my own village there are periodical outbreaks when street names are removed and nothing in a front garden seems safe. This should not deter people from having decorative features, but it is as well to remember that anything small and portable is liable to disappear unless it can be securely fastened or cemented in place.

Plants suffer least, and established shrubs are not easy to

pull up. A varied group of shrubs provides a good screen
between house and road without the rigidity of a hedge. The
shrubs need to be well-spaced and carefully chosen for contrast,
and a good proportion of evergreens (and greys and yellows)
will ensure that the garden looks cheerful and 'furnished' when
neighbouring ones may be winter-bare and drab. One such
shrub-bed I know contains a purple prunus, a *Cryptomeria
japonica Elegans* (a bushy conifer which is green in summer and
bronze in winter), a variegated holly, a shiny green *Hebe* with
purple flowers (Midsummer Beauty) and a smaller one with
white flowers and bluish foliage, a golden form of Lawson's
cypress, a lavender bush, and a sizeable clump of bergenia,
which flowers in January. There are groups of spring bulbs

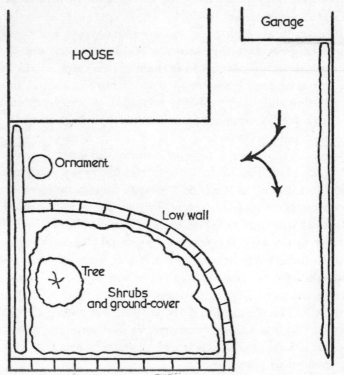

Front garden for privacy and easy maintenance

here and there between the shrubs; and edging plants such as bugle, aubrietia and pinks partly mask the low wall (three bricks high) which retains the shrub-bed and prevents anyone from driving on to it. Altogether it is a very successful planting and it looks well-groomed and thriving whatever the time of year.

There is a sad dearth of trees in many housing developments, so a handsome one in a front garden gives distinction to a house and pleasure to many people besides its owner. Laburnum, rowan, red may and flowering cherry are the commonest trees in suburban gardens, but it is worth looking for something unusual. Two small gardens I look for at the appropriate time of year contain respectively a magnolia and a cherry. The magnolia is not the more widely planted (but very beautiful) white one, but *Magnolia lennei*, whose huge waxen flowers are purple outside and white within. The cherry is the winter-flowering *Prunus subhirtella Autumnalis*. Magnolias are slow developers but they are worth waiting for, especially the unusual pink-flowered kinds like *M. cambellii*. I feel that the pink cherry called Kanzan, with bronze young leaves, is overplanted because the tree is an ugly shape, like an umbrella blown inside out, and one must live with it all the year, not just when the abundant blossom makes it acceptable. There is one with white tutus dancing on long stalks: a prettier, more spreading tree. It is called *Prunus serrulata Longipes* or, sometimes, Shimidsu Sakura.

The best plan is to visit a tree nursery or arboretum, or some of the gardens open to the public (booklets containing addresses and dates are on sale at large newsagents) and note the names of suitably sized trees which catch your eye. It is wise to go at different seasons to get a fair picture. You might end up with a Handkerchief Tree (*Davidia involucrata*)—the 'hankies' are not petals but large bracts around the flowers—or a fast-growing eucalyptus (*E. gunnii*) which has round blue leaves when small and longer sage-green ones later. You could have a silver-splashed conifer, or even a bed of assorted conifers—tall and

thin, conical, billowy, bun-shaped or prostrate—in various
colours. Or your choice might be a quince or Bird Cherry, a
weeping willow-leafed pear, a medlar, a Corkscrew hazel or one
with purple or yellow foliage; it might be a *Ginkgo*, a deciduous
cone-bearing tree whose nearest relatives lived in Britain about
the time when coal was being formed. Its unusual leaves turn
a glorious clear yellow in autumn. Then there is the delightfully
named *Liquidambar*—*L. orientalis* is smaller than the American
Sweet Gum, *L. styraciflua*. Or you could choose a mulberry, or
one of the less common varieties of rowan such as *Sorbus
aucuparia Xanthocarpa* with yellow berries or *S. hupehensis* with
white ones. For the pleasure of passers-by as well as your own,
a Chinese witch-hazel would fit into the smallest garden. This
is *Hamamelis mollis*, and it bears its unusual and very fragrant
flowers from December to February. The species whose bark
and leaf-shoots are the source of commercial 'witch-hazel' is an
attractive little tree called *H. virginiana*. One thinks of beeches,
elms and maples as huge trees, but all of them have less common
smaller-growing varieties. Dickson's Golden Elm is very slow,
with bright golden foliage all the year not just in autumn.
Fagus grandiflora is an American beech, which never reaches the
dimensions of the British native kind. The Japanese Maple (*Acer
palmatum*) is a small tree, though its many varieties tend to
remain shrublike. The striking Snake-bark Maple (*A. penn-
sylvanicum*) is another of reasonable size.

These trees may not be available at the nearest garden centre,
but it is worth a little effort to have a tree which is more
interesting and 'different'. It may be more expensive, but it is
better to pay for one tree which really appeals to you than to
buy three cheap, commonplace ones. The search for and choice
of it will contribute to the pleasure of having it.

Next, having chosen its site, plant the tree with every
consideration given to its likes and dislikes, and avoid planting
anything close to it which will hide its glories and prevent it
from flourishing as it should. It does not have to be in the
centre of the plot, nor in the centre of the cultivated patch. Try

to imagine it in ten years' time, to see how it will look in relation to the road and what is beyond from indoors, and also in relation to the house seen from the road. Where there is room for a tree at both sides of the plot (that is, where the garage approach does not, as so often happens, run close against the side boundary), two trees can make a charming frame for a house. They need not be the same kind; indeed it will be more interesting if, for instance, a tall narrow conifer were contrasted with a low-branched spreading or weeping tree. Or two which will be at their most interesting at different seasons of the year might be chosen. Nurserymen sometimes sell what they regard as misshapen trees, ones which fork low down or lean to one side, but these often have more character than those with a straight stem and they are usually cheaper.

Variation in levels lends interest to the dullest piece of ground, so the tree might be planted on an artificial mound. It depends on what is to be done with the ground beneath. Grass, perhaps planted with bulbs for a spring display, is easier to cut if it is level. A mound is better covered with a carpeter which can be sheared flat once a year. Creeping thyme, or that Elizabethan favourite, camomile, or heathers (of which there are winter- and summer-flowering types) are all suitable. A low retaining wall of the kind previously suggested for a shrub-bed could also be used where there is a specimen tree. The remainder of the bed could be planted with ground-cover, of all one sort or in large irregular patches of different kinds which will knit into a weed-defying mat. Rose of Sharon, bugle, periwinkle, pachysandra, bergenia and violets do well even in shade; pinks and irises (good for gardens on lime), Lamb's Ears, santolina and the pink-flowered, shamrock-leafed *Oxalis floribunda* need adequate sunlight.

It is surprising that many people who go to a lot of trouble in selecting colour schemes for their houses seldom think of extending them to include the garden. A one-colour theme— or two-colour since there will almost always be some green— could be tedious on a large scale, but it would be unusual and

eye-catching and fun to work out in a small front garden.
Coloured foliage gives the longest-lasting effects. 'The house
with the white and silver front garden' could become a local
landmark. Begin with a silvery tree—a weeping pear, or
Chamaecyparis Boulevard, or whitebeam, whose opening leaf-buds
have the look of greenish-silver magnolia blooms. Continue
with shrubs like lavender, senecio and artemisia, and carpeters
like stachys and santolina, Snow-in-Summer and arabis. White-
flowered bulbs such as snowdrops and crocuses, and summer-
flowering galtonias, snowflakes (*Leucojum*), and regal and
Madonna lilies would need no attention. There would be no
need to have annual or herbaceous plants.

A greeny golden scheme could be planned using a yellow-
leafed tree or golden conifer; variegated and golden shrubs
from privet to *Elaeagnus*; golden marjoram, variegated periwinkles and ivies, Creeping Jenny and *Sedum acre* as ground-
cover; and daffodils, yellow alyssum and golden mounds of
broom and hypericum to reinforce the sunny effect.

A pale stone or rendered house might be enhanced by a
setting of crimson and purple-leafed plants: look for words like
atropurpurea and *rubrifolia* in the botanical description. There are
purple-leafed maples and filberts, malus and prunus varieties,
and the spectacular purple Smoke Tree, *Cotinus coggygria Foliis
Purpureis*. The various 'purple willows' do not have purple
leaves: the name applies to the stems and young shoots. Some
are kept pollarded in the same way as the crimson-stemmed
dogwoods, and both give a glow of colour in the winter. The
weeping purple willow is a very attractive small tree. Dwarf
Prunus cistena has effective red shoots and makes a good flowering
hedge, breathtaking if the setting sun shines through it. This is
true of many red-leafed plants. On a dull day they dwindle to
a purplish-brown, but lit by the sun they glow splendidly and
repay careful placing. Other suitable shrubs are purple sage,
Berberis thunbergii atropurpurea (*nana* is the dwarf form, about 2ft
each way), and *Rosa rubrifolia* which makes a 5ft bush covered
with single pink roses in summer. A vine with leaves which

mature from red to purple can be trained on the house wall: this is *Vitis vinifera Purpurea*. As well as bugle, suitable ground-cover plants include an unusual violet called *Viola labradorica purpurea* and purple forms of stonecrop and houseleek. Some of these crimson and purple plants could be mixed with greys and silvers to produce really splendid harmonies, and other combinations can be worked out. One-colour borders can be seen in many gardens which are open to the public, such as the National Trust gardens of Sissinghurst Castle in Kent and Tintinhull in Somerset, and they are a useful source of ideas.

A front garden also makes a successful herb garden. The simplest way is to pave it all, setting the slabs in concrete where the car will run on them but leaving random planting spaces elsewhere. It could also be laid out chess-board fashion, alternating each slab with a square patch of one herb, or in some other formal layout such as narrow parallel borders. Even the concrete cul-de-sac for turning the car could be fitted into the pattern with a little ingenuity, and given point by means of a formal clipped bay tree in a pot at the farther end. The more formal the layout, the neater the plants should be kept, but this is not arduous. The combination of herbs and paving is ideal, as sprigs for flavouring are close to hand and can be picked at any time without getting one's feet wet. The essentials for happy herbs are sunshine and good drainage. The only herbs which like damp, shady conditions are the invasive members of the mint family. If these are to be included, confine them to pots or sunken buckets (bottomless or with drainage holes) and remember to water them. A herb garden is a pleasant place to linger in on a sunny day, so add a small seat if there is room.

A small garden with a high proportion of paving like this also makes a good setting for a collection of plants which reflect the owner's particular interest. It might be one family like irises or primulas; or something more esoteric, such as a collection of the plants mentioned in Shakespeare's plays. Discovering these would be a cultural as well as a horticultural

exercise. A reference book can be obtained. Plants which are
interesting when examined closely, but less effective in a wider
context, are a good choice for a small garden, where they will
not be overlooked. The blue passion-flower, *Passiflora caerulea*,
is an example. It has unusual and beautiful flowers which come
in small numbers all summer and not in one eye-catching
burst. A climber, it needs a warm wall if it is to flourish. The
yellow clematis varieties like *Clematis tangutica* and the thick-
petalled *C. orientalis* (sometimes called the Orange-peel
Clematis) are not as spectacular as the large-flowered hybrids,
but their nodding flowers are pretty and are followed by
attractive, fluffy seed-pods which last into the winter.

Passion-flower,
Passiflora caerulea

A front garden which is permanently in shadow poses a
different problem. A tree will grow towards the light but will
add to the difficulties of whatever is planted at its base. Ground-
cover plants which thrive in shade have been mentioned, but
the most interesting of all shade-lovers are the ferns. They
could be the main feature of a moist, shady front garden, and
it would certainly be unusual. Some are evergreen; some have
solid leaves and others lacy ones; many turn to rich rusty tones

in autumn. They are woodland plants, so the soil should be well dug and enriched with plenty of humus such as rotted leaves, compost, peat or spent hops. They do not thrive on chalk or heavy clays, but there are some small ones which exist without apparent nourishment in the stone walls of Devon and Somerset. The pretty Lady fern (*Athyrium filix-femina*) is fascinating from the time its fronds begin to unfurl in spring until they form a perfect shuttlecock about 3ft high. There are many variations with more cut, curly or mossy fronds. The Male fern, *Dryopteris filix-mas*, is similar but more robust. Hart's Tongue fern is quite different, with very long and narrow evergreen leaves which contrast effectively with the feathery kinds. Its name is *Phyllitis scolopendrium*. Larger, and requiring a very damp spot if it is to flourish, *Osmunda regalis* is the Royal fern, a majestic plant which may reach 5ft. It colours splendidly in autumn. An elegant evergreen with 3ft fronds is *Polystichum setigerum*, while *Cryptogramma crispa* is only 6in high and resembles very curly parsley at first sight. Like several other ferns it has two distinct kinds of frond, fertile and sterile. Ferns do not have seeds but reproduce from spores carried on the backs of some leaves. There are many other kinds and countless different forms of those named. Most ferns are easy to grow if the conditions are right. Many will increase in size and beauty for up to twenty years, with no more attention than the removal of last year's leaves and an annual top dressing of wood-ash, peat or leaf mould.

Some older front gardens have been reduced to virtual invisibility by road-widening schemes, and more and more new houses have nothing in front but open-plan grass cut into sections with repetitious concrete. One wonders whether the front garden is doomed to extinction along with the carriage drive and the formal parterre. It would be a pity. House design nowadays has a depressing sameness about it and the front garden offers the owner some chance to express his individuality, to make his home a little different from his neighbour's, and to benefit everyone by contributing more visual interest to his surroundings.

Chapter 6

Informal Fruit Gardens

ONE SIMPLE WAY of dealing with a plot of land is to grass it over and plant it as an orchard, adding one or two fruit trees whenever funds allow. A hedge of hazel could enclose it and yield nuts as well. There are many advantages: an orchard makes a suitable setting for a cottage or cottagelike, small modern house; it allows playing space for children; it costs very little; and it produces fruit three or four years after planting. Maintenance would be limited to cutting the grass, and a necessary minimum of feeding and pruning. For a beginner it also means that only one simple book on fruit-growing will be needed for reference, not a huge tome covering roses and shrubs and alpines and lawn-maintenance. . .

The effect of fruit trees grown in straight lines may not appeal, but the idea of a simple, productive, easily kept garden does. There is no reason at all why the ground should not be laid out in an informal manner while still being devoted to fruit-growing. It simply means that the garden would be planned as a garden but that the trees, shrubs, hedging and climbers used would all bear edible fruit. It would look nice without constant attention and would suit working couples and retired people alike. The fruit would come as a welcome bonus.

Even the smallest garden (perhaps 20ft × 20ft), so long as it is not heavily shaded, could accommodate one bush or dwarf pyramid apple tree with another variety for pollination trained as cordon or espalier against the fence or house wall. There

would be room too for a small bed of Alpine strawberries, and
for gooseberries or redcurrants or a fan-trained Morello cherry
on the remaining vertical surfaces. A bigger garden gives more
scope, but care should be taken to avoid overcrowding as this
reduces the yield and encourages disease.

Grass could be lawn or the rougher kind cut once a month
with a rotary mower. There would be no clipped hedges.
Hazel makes an effective tall screen, bearing catkins in early
spring and nuts in autumn. For the best nuts, trees should be
obtained from a nurseryman rather than from a wild hedgerow
(which is illegal). Cobnuts and filberts are similar. These
bushes throw up suckers, and though this helps to form a hedge,
they should not be allowed to become a thicket taking up too
much space and making picking difficult. The suckers should
be cut neatly through the thickening at the base and, if required,
they will root readily to increase your stock. They thrive best
on a light soil and do not make such dense growth.

A single tree, grown on one stem with all suckers removed,
looks decorative and is a suitable size for any garden. Kentish
Cob is a good variety, bearing very long male catkins which
are most attractive in February. It produces a heavy crop of
well-flavoured nuts. Cosford is another good one, but Kentish
Filbert is less suitable as a specimen tree because the male
catkins are few, though the crop is abundant. Pick the nuts
when the shells are hard and spread them on a floor or shelf,
turning them over once or twice as they dry. They can be
stored in a cool place until Christmas, but make sure it is
mouseproof!

An alternative hedge could be the colourful Japanese quince,
Chaenomeles (or *Cydonia*) *speciosa*. This will grow to 8ft tall and
bears white, pink or scarlet blossom according to the variety.
Many people know this shrub as 'japonica' and regard it as
purely ornamental, but the stalkless yellow fruit is edible. Too
hard to eat raw, it makes an incomparable jelly of rich flavour
and attractive colour. The flowers may come from January
onwards, with the main flush in April. As it fruits on the old

wood, it benefits by having the young growth trimmed back in August and again during the winter: this will keep it neat. It soon builds up a strong network of branches with enough spines to form an effective barrier against livestock and small boys. A dwarf variety, up to 3ft, is *C. japonica* which has flame-coloured flowers and similar fruit. This quince is tolerant of most soils and thrives as a hedge or against a wall even in shade. Grown in the open it is among the most beautiful of early-flowering shrubs. Sloes and bullaces might also be planted as a tall wind-break for a larger garden.

There may be fencing around the garden. There will certainly be house, and probably garage, walls. All will look better with something growing on them: all provide favoured conditions for tender plants. A sunny, south-facing fence or wall is a good place for a fan-trained peach, apricot or nectarine. The tree will already be well-shaped if it is bought as a three-year-old. These all flower early in the year and although they are all self-fertile, there are few insects about in cold weather and the blossom may be damaged by frost before pollination. Artificial pollination is carried out by gently passing a camel-hair brush or rabbit's tail over the flowers to transfer pollen from one to another.

All these fruit trees need a good, well-drained soil and the bed for them against the wall should be carefully prepared, with lime added in some form, preferably old mortar. Apricots, which grow twice as fast as peaches, are a little more fussy and for them a light soil would need stiffening with loam and manure, without spoiling the drainage. Plant the tree about 9in from the wall, spreading the roots fanwise in front and checking that the soil-mark is in the same place as it was in the nursery. The branches are tied to wires run along the wall, but held an inch or so away from it with battens or vine-eyes to discourage red spider. A mature tree will occupy about 15ft of horizontal wall-space, so allow for this. The best planting time is November. Remember that the ground at the base of a south wall tends to be dry. During the summer the tree will benefit from watering and mulching. Nectarines in particular need plenty of water when the crop starts to swell. Wait until the early-summer drop is over before thinning the fruit. First remove one of any 'twins', then any fruits pressing against the wall and any others which are too close, leaving 4in between apricots and 9in between peaches and nectarines. Moorpark is the apricot most grown in Britain; Early Rivers, Elruge and Pineapple are reliable nectarines; Amsden June and Peregrine are good peaches. In mild districts in southern England, peaches can be grown as bushes in the open. Nectarines are not hardy enough. When the fruits are ripening, little bags of muslin or nylon stocking may be put over them and tied to the branches, to foil wasps and to catch them when they fall.

Another possibility for a south-facing wall is a grape-vine, which will need trellis or wires to climb on. Planting in over-rich soil tends to produce a lot of leaf at the expense of fruit, and vines should not be mulched. Being deep-rooted they seldom need watering after the first year. Vines are hardy, but they need plenty of sun for the fruit to develop and ripen properly. In a poor summer the grapes may be small, especially if the bunches have not been thinned, but they can be used to make a pleasant wine. In any case the leaves are decorative, and one can console oneself for a poor crop with that Continental delicacy, stuffed vine-leaves. A reliable nurseryman would recommend the best variety for your district but Brandt (black), Buckland Sweetwater and Royal Muscadine (white) have a good reputation outdoors.

Espalier apples or pears would also flourish on a south-facing wall, but they do equally well on a west one. Espaliers need to be about 15ft apart but cordons, which are single stems trained to an angle of 45°, can be put in 2½ft apart, and are easier for an amateur to train and prune. A fan-trained dessert plum would also be a good choice for a west-facing wall. East and north walls are less attractive, but I have seen a very good Conference pear against an east-facing wall, and fan-trained Morello cherries do well on north ones. This is a cooking cherry and self-fertile, so only one need be grown. It will need 12–15ft of horizontal wall-space. Japanese quince will thrive against any wall and needs little support, but it does need careful training in the early stages to build up a flat framework of branches over the area the shrub is expected to cover. Later on, only exuberant new growths need trimming back.

Blackberries and loganberries may also be grown on fences. Either will need a 10ft run of fence with wires stretched along it about 12in apart, the lowest 2ft above ground. Both are trouble-free and tolerant of most soils, and choosing a thornless variety will eliminate their only drawback. Blackberries are juicier when grown in semi-shade, but loganberries prefer an open, sunny position. Old fruited canes should be cut out after harvesting and the new canes which have grown during the summer should be tied in their place. Oregon Thornless is a prickle-free blackberry with excellent fruit. The Thornless loganberry is not as vigorous as the true loganberry but it is of course easier to train. Loganberries are greedy plants and they appreciate liberal doses of compost. Blackberries also benefit from an occasional mulch.

Surprisingly enough, gooseberries and redcurrants can also be grown on walls and fences, even north-facing ones, trained as vertical cordons on wires or trellis. They are useful because they will fit between or under windows where nothing else will. Plant three-year-old cordons 2ft apart, preferably in November. Redcurrants do best in a light soil and will not thrive where drainage is poor. A mulch of straw will keep the base free from weeds and a dressing of fish manure each February will encourage fruit production. Gooseberries prefer a heavier soil, and benefit from a mulch of compost. Red Lake is a fruitful currant and Keepsake and Lancashire Lad are reliable gooseberries. A big advantage of growing these against a wall or fence is the ease with which they can be draped with netting to protect them from birds.

Having dealt with the vertical surfaces, we can consider trees. Although they need not be planted in rows, it is still vital

Beehives in a small orchard

Beekeeper examining combs

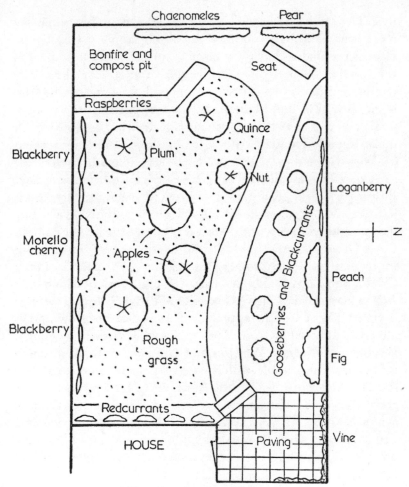

Informal layout for a fruit garden

to give them as much space as they would be allowed in an orchard. For apples and pears this means 8–10ft apart for dwarf pyramids, 12–18ft for bushes, and 30–40ft for half or full standards. The smaller trees are suitable for modern gardens and are easier to prune, spray and pick. Two small trees are better than one large, because each should have a pollinator flowering at the same time. A good nursery will advise about

F

this. The choice of apple varieties is enormous but some are more ornamental than others. A cooking apple called Upton Pyne is reputed to have the most beautiful blossom of all, but the variety called Arthur Turner must run it very close. The clustered crimson buds open to large pink flowers and the fruit is big, beautiful and abundant. It is usable from July to September but does not keep, which is a drawback. However, it makes superlative apple purée for bottling. Another excellent cooker is Grenadier, which produces large, flattish apples very early on a compact little tree. Where spring frosts are common, Edward VII is a good cooker to grow as it flowers late and is less likely to be nipped. The large green apples have a fine flavour and will keep until April if properly stored. At its best, Cox's Orange Pippin is a splendid dessert apple, but it is not the easiest apple to grow well. Another fine eater is James Grieve, and Lord Lambourne is a first-class variety which does well in many places where Cox will not thrive. Ellison's Orange is rather like a Cox in appearance. It is easy to grow and is almost unaffected by frost. Two apples which have exceptional keeping qualities are Winston and Granny Smith. Winston is a firm, red juicy apple which hangs on to the tree even after leaf-fall, and stores well until April. As it flowers late, it is a good choice for districts where spring frosts occur. Granny Smith is really an Australian apple, large, green and juicy, and at its best when there is a long hot summer. I seldom pick mine until November: stored in a cool dry place they are still firm and tasty the following May.

These are only a personal selection from the hundreds available. The wisest thing to do is to visit the best fruit nursery in your area, explain your preferences, and ask advice. The nurseryman will tell you what varieties especially suit your soil, which are available as espaliers and which pollinate each other. It is worth buying the best trees, even if you buy only one at a time, because cheap stock is nearly always a disappointment. In theory, the 'family' trees so widely advertised are an attractive idea for a small garden. Three main branches of three different varieties are grafted on to a single rootstock so that they pollinate each other and three sorts of apple are obtained. In practice, the different parts of the tree often grow at different speeds and one more vigorous branch can exhaust the other two. Hard pruning of the dominant one encourages still stronger growth, often at the expense of fruit. The usual result is an ugly, unbalanced tree and the crop is generally just as unsatisfactory.

The main requirement for apple trees is well-drained soil. They do not thrive, and may actually die, in water-logged ground. A stake should be put in when planting, otherwise winds will rock the young tree and the new small roots it is trying to put out will be continually broken. There are several kinds of tie, but whatever sort is used, check them often and slacken them when necessary. A tree can make a sudden spurt in growth and a tight string will soon eat deeply into the bark.

Pears are not difficult to grow, but they prefer soil which does not dry out in summer. Some pears, notably Conference, will produce a crop when planted alone, but the majority need a pollinator. Unless there is a suitable variety just over your garden fence, it is advisable to have two trees. Conference is an easy one and William's Bon Chrétien is a good pollen partner for it. So is the reliable and delicious Baronne de Mello. Louise Bonne of Jersey is an early-flowering pear with beautiful blossom and prolific fruit. Packham's Triumph is a possible pollinator and this variety makes a very small tree, suitable for a modern garden. The fruit is like a William. Standard and half-standard pears take a long time to come into bearing, so buy dwarf pyramids or bushes. Where space is limited the second tree can be an espalier against the house wall or fence.

Plum trees are never dwarf because no suitable stock is known, but bush plums are a reasonable size, and they can also be bought fan-trained for a wall. There are several self-fertile varieties of plum, which is convenient if you have room for one only. The well-known dessert plum Victoria and the reliable and frost-resistant Giant Prune are two of them.

Pershore Yellow Egg, the best yellow cooking plum, is also self-fertile. Among plums we must include those traditional fruits of cottage gardens which seldom seem to reach the shops: greengages and damsons. The Old Greengage (Reine Claude) bears delicious fruit but is not such a heavy or reliable cropper as the Cambridge Gage, though the latter needs a pollinator. Merryweather Damson is a hardy, self-fertile and prolific sort. Should you want a weeping fruit tree for your garden, it is among the plums that you will find it. Many varieties have this tendency, but the most 'weepy' of all is called the Warwickshire Drooper. Despite this lethargic name, it is one of the best late plums and gives regular and heavy crops. It is self-fertile too. All plums prefer a rich soil with some lime added.

I do not think sweet cherries are a practical proposition for any small garden. They need a good deal of space and, as none is self-fertile, two must be planted. They are fussy about soil and slow to start fruiting, and when they do, the fruit is liable to be stripped by birds unless the branches have been covered with netting in good time. Fan-trained trees can be bought but they do not seem to crop very well. A Morello cherry is a more hopeful prospect. Either as a bush or fan-trained, it produces a good crop of very dark red cherries, and though the fruit is sour eaten raw it makes splendid pies, jam and brandied cherries. The bushes should be planted 18ft apart. They are best grown in cultivated ground, not in grass, but a mulch of straw sprinkled with fish fertiliser in February will keep down weeds and conserve moisture. Morellos need plenty of water while the fruit is developing.

Apple, pear, plum and cherry are the fruit trees we usually think of, but there are less common ones which will add variety and interest. Figs have been grown in England since at least the time of Henry VIII. To fruit well they need a sunny south or west wall, very poor soil, and restriction of their roots. I have sometimes thought that a fig tree would be best planted in a filled-in well, but a hole 3ft square lined on all sides with concrete or sheets of galvanised iron is usually recommended.

The bottom should be of broken bricks and no manure should be added to the soil. Fruits begin to form as buds on the tips of the young wood one year and swell the next summer. The second-crop figs never swell in temperate climates as the summers are too short. They should be picked off in November, as they may inhibit the formation of the next year's fruit. The buds may need the protection of sacking draped over them in a harsh winter. Brown Turkey is a very hardy and prolific fig.

Another luscious fruit seldom seen today is the mulberry. Some very old trees can be seen in the grounds of historic houses, but their age is often exaggerated because they begin to look very ancient while still quite young. No tree has more

Mulberry,
Morus nigra

character than the mulberry. Though not really large, it does need space because of its curious tendency to lie down. It has a heavy head, and many trees soon develop a pronounced lean. Old ones are often seen with stout props holding them up. This may be thought a drawback, but the ripe fruit will compensate for all the tree's eccentricities. Delicious when eaten raw, it can also be cooked. It has a slight tartness, and the rich dark juice swirls sumptuously into the cream. I remember that our tree was out of bounds to us when we were children because the juice stained our clothes and faces. Birds knock down more mulberries than they eat, so old, clean sheets should be spread out under the tree to catch the fruit. As a specimen tree it is ideal, perhaps for the front garden, in an area of grass. Though not fussy about soil, it does respond to good treatment.

Quinces could be grown far more as ornamental trees. I have the variety Vranja, which produces large pink flowers followed by pear-shaped golden fruit as downy as a peach. The young leaves are furry too. Meech's Prolific is a reliable variety with smooth-skinned fruit. Quinces make a delicious jelly and one added to an apple pie improves the flavour surprisingly. Medlars are also attractive small trees, bearing big white blossoms in May and June; but the fruit is an acquired taste. Medlars are eaten semi-rotten or 'bletted', and Victorian gentlemen enjoyed them with their after-dinner port. In appearance they resemble nothing so much as a very large, flattened, brown rose-hip, which is not surprising because the tree (*Mespilus germanica*) belongs to the family Rosaceae. So does the well-known rowan, which is also a fruit tree. Rowan jelly is an excellent accompaniment to game and rich meats. Use 2lb of berries to 1lb of tart cooking apples. Crab-apples (*Malus*) are useful and ornamental small trees: John Downie especially has colourful and abundant fruit. There is a most attractive semi-weeping form of the wild hedgerow crab-apple, *Malus pumila*, called *Pendula*, which also bears good fruit.

In a sheltered place where the blossom will not be frost-bitten, an almond tree is very pretty and will produce plenty of nuts. *Prunus amygdalus* has chalky, pale pink blossoms: its variety *Praecox* is similar but it flowers a week or two earlier and may need artificial pollination. Almonds do well in most soils but heavy clay needs to be well-drained. On acid soil a dressing of lime will be beneficial. 'Peach-leaf curl' is an ugly disease liable to attack peaches and almonds. Spraying with a suitable fungicide in mid-February, and again two weeks later, is a wise precaution. Nuts can be left until they fall, unless squirrels are likely to steal them: if so, pick them in October. Walnuts are beautiful trees, but they are so large and take so long to begin cropping that they do not suit modern gardens. Some nurserymen supply grafted bushes, which are said to be more satisfactory. Avoid planting them in hollows and low places where frost collects, as this will spoil the flowers. Higher ground may seem more exposed but frost drains downhill and will cause less damage. Franquette is a reliable French walnut; the large oval nut has a comparatively unwrinkled shell.

Now to the shrubs, which is what most soft-fruits are. These can be grown in a bed or along the sides of a path, but not in grass. Careless and Leveller are fine green gooseberries to grow as bushes in an open position. They can grow on quite a long 'leg' which makes weeding under them—and picking—less painful. Whinham's Industry is a red hairy berry which does fairly well under trees. Blackcurrants grow from a 'stool'. After the third year most of the old wood should be cut out after harvesting, and the new branches which grow from the base during the summer carry the next year's crop. Blackcurrants prefer a damp, rich soil and will tolerate some shade if they are well-fed. Laxton's Giant and Amos Black are good varieties, one early and one late. These bush fruits each need a space about 5ft square, though they could be kept smaller by pruning. Red and white currants differ from black in that they are grown on a leg, and the fruit is produced on old wood. A redcurrant can be grown as a half-standard on a 3–4ft stem. It looks very ornamental, as well as being easy to pick. However, birds find the fruit irresistible and in most areas netting will be needed for protection. Laxton's No 1 is a productive mid-season currant with good colour, and White Versailles bears large sweet berries in abundance. White currants are seldom available in the shops. This is a pity, since they make a really luscious summer dessert.

Raspberries are useful as an internal hedge, perhaps to screen the bonfire or compost heap Plant them 12in apart.

To keep them tidy, put two posts 15in apart at each end of the row and run wires, bamboo canes or wooden battens down both sides. A long row may need two or three lengths of twine linking the wires across the row at intervals. Dig all perennial weeds out of the ground before planting because it is almost impossible to eradicate things like couch-grass afterwards. Raspberries need good drainage but must not dry out in summer, so a liberal mulch of straw put down after planting and added to each year as the worms pull it down will conserve moisture, suppress weeds and feed the plants. Apply a good sprinkling of bone-meal or fish manure over the straw in February. After they have fruited, cut out all the old canes, leaving the strong young ones to take their place for the following year.

Where the soil is acid, several unusual berries can be grown. So long as the ground is not water-logged, the cranberry will thrive. This is an evergreen trailer bearing red berries which are used to make jelly. It is often happy when planted beside a stream. The bilberry or huckleberry enjoys similar conditions. This is a deciduous shrub growing about 12in high with purple berries. In damp, acid places the North American shrub called the blueberry (*Vaccinium corymbosum*) may do well (and who has not heard of blueberry pie?). This makes a bigger bush, eventually about 6ft high, with pretty flowers and brilliant autumn leaf-colour.

Strawberries are not suitable for informal treatment, with the exception of the bush or alpine strawberry, Baron Sole-macher, which does not throw out runners. This is an attractive plant which does best in semi-shade in a humus-rich soil. The little strawberries are abundant for several weeks from August onwards and are delicious when eaten raw. For jam-making the fruit has the advantage of 'setting' readily without added pectin.

The pruning of fruit trees differs from species to species and really needs diagrams to make the methods clear. The gardener who is devoting his plot to fruit should buy one of the excellent

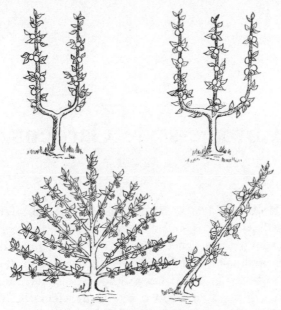

Some shapes of trained fruit trees

text-books which deal with pruning, pests and diseases and other relevant subjects. If you discover in yourself a talent for training fruit trees, you may want to progress beyond the fan-trained peach and the espalier on the fence. Interesting features can be created. Espalier apples and pears can be trained along the sides of paths, as can oblique cordons, U-cordons and double U-cordons. The text-book of your choice will explain this in detail. There is also a most decorative Belgian system of training, *l'arcure*, in which branches arch alternately to right and left. Cordon pears can be trained over iron arches to form a living pergola or tunnel over a path. The French have a particular gift for this sort of artistry. But, however fascinating, it is something which needs regular if not very arduous attention, and it is not wise to start unless you are going to keep it up. For most people the simple layout is best, but the beauty of the idea is that it can be just as elaborate as time and taste dictate, and all ways offer the bonus of fresh fruit to enjoy.

Chapter 7

Cottage-style Gardens

THERE IS tremendous romance and nostalgia about cottage gardens, but the truth is that the real cottage garden was a kitchen-garden. We have a mental picture of a little hedge-encircled plot overflowing with flowers, a thatched cottage in the background, and a winding path leading to a front door framed in purple clematis. This is a long way from the truth. Unless they were essential on account of searing winds, cottagers seldom grew hedges which robbed the soil of nourishment and further reduced the size of the plot. There were no winding paths, because the shortest route to the door was the most sensible one. Flowers were less important than food, and the purple clematis was not introduced into England before 1860. Cottagers were not romantic people with an eye to picturesque effect. Life was too hard for indulging in flights of fancy, and the delightful effect often achieved was accidental. Gardens were crammed in that charming way because the cottager had to get all he could from his bit of ground: it was economic necessity.

Overflowing abundance, and the mixing together of flowers, fruit and vegetables are the two outstanding characteristics of cottage gardens. That necessary overcrowding was made possible by the lavish use of animal manures, to which the cottager had easy access. He probably kept a pig, cow or donkey himself, as well as rabbits and poultry. Plants do better growing close together so long as they have room to develop

100

and the ground is kept in good heart. Weeds are suppressed and moisture is conserved. The cottager's rows of cabbages and beans would have needed hoeing only when young: soon each would fill its allotted space.

The idea that flowers and vegetables were grown higgledy-piggledy together probably arose from a misapprehension. Cottagers grew numerous herbs for culinary and medicinal purposes, and also for 'sweet bags' to keep moths away from stored Sunday clothes and to scent linen. Many of these herbs bore flowers: in some it was the flowers which had the valuable properties. To a sophisticated passer-by it might seem that flowers and vegetables were growing together. To the cottager there was no plant in the garden which was not, first and foremost, useful. The giant sunflowers might look decorative but the seeds would feed poultry in the winter and the leaves were fodder for the cow. Lavender, rosemary and woodruff were for bags and pot-pourri, vital to combat the mustiness of a damp cottage. Borage and bergamot, tansy, sage, mint and marigolds, pinks and primroses had culinary uses. Hyssop and mallow yielded cough mixtures, a tisane of violet leaves cured a headache, camomile induced sleep, foxgloves were used to stimulate a tired heart (and stopped it altogether if the brew were too strong). Pyrethrum and pennyroyal destroyed fleas and loosestrife discouraged flies. Elecampane's shaggy daisies, gaudy nasturtiums, even the older roses were not there to make the garden pretty. That they did so was entirely a matter of chance.

If there were a tree in the garden it would be a fruit tree, generally an apple because the fruit was abundant and versatile and could be stored for winter use. We can have little notion of how austere life was for a cottager in the wintertime. There might be a grass plot under the tree, and if so a beehive would stand there since honey was the cheapest sweetening agent available. More commonly, the ground would be planted with whatever crops could be expected to thrive. As dwarfing stocks were uncommon in those days, the tree would be a standard, so a good deal of light and air would penetrate underneath the branches.

Later on some plants were undoubtedly grown for their scent and colour; and perhaps some for the bees. A root of honeysuckle brought in from the hedgerow or the wild clematis called Traveller's Joy or Old Man's Beard might be trained upon rustic poles round the door or over the gate. Almost the only other climber used was the colourful and prolific runner-bean, usually grown on the fence. Most early cottage-garden flowers must have been naturalised from the wild or been acquired from the herb gardens of the monasteries after the Dissolution. Later, as the whims of fashion caused changes in the manor and 'big house' gardens, more exotic roots and cuttings would come the way of the cottage-dweller. Many of the plants we think of as 'cottagey' are comparatively recent arrivals. Lilac, sunflowers, Crown Imperials and philadelphus reached England in the seventeenth century; flowering currant, clarkia and nemophila not until the nineteenth. And there were no roses round the door until at least the eighteenth century, unless they were wild ones, because climbers as we know them were latecomers and at first were available only to the wealthy.

The cottage-type garden is a suitable one to have today, for several reasons. It is not difficult to maintain once it is established, and as land-values increase, gardens are becoming smaller. Moreover, many modern houses of traditional design are 'cottagey' in appearance and look well set in a gay, thickly planted garden. It must be said that whereas almost any plant blends pleasantly with the whitewashed rendering or weathered brick of a genuine old cottage, modern materials are seldom as sympathetic. Some modern bricks are very harsh in tone and care should be taken as to what is planted close to them. Climbers or shrubs with white or cream-coloured flowers and abundant greenery will often be found best to soften hard lines and crude colouring.

It would be difficult to reproduce anything like a typical old cottage garden. We would be self-consciously striving after a certain effect: the real cottager grew what he needed, unconcerned about any effect. However, what we really want is not a genuine cottage garden but something closer to the romantic flowery paradise we think of as being a cottage garden.

I once knew an octogenarian with a very odd garden—the last genuine cottage garden in his village, I should think. A narrow path ran down one side and the entire ground was planted in rows except where something of a permanent nature such as a fruit tree, lavender bush or old cabbage rose happened to be. It was not all vegetables; there was a row of pansies between the carrots and the onions, a wide belt of pinks between the runner-beans and the strawberries, and common old-fashioned marigolds next to the lettuce. At the far end an elder tree, honeysuckle, and jasmine obscured the privy. Middle-class owners have modernised the cottage and made something more like our dream cottage garden—but old Mark's garden was the real thing.

Whether to have vegetables or not is a question to be settled at the beginning. Some people claim that a kitchen-garden can look as attractive as a flower-bed, and they produce photographs to prove it. Neat rows of lettuce, feathery-topped carrots and red-leafed beets do look attractive. The frilly green of Salad Bowl lettuce makes it one of the prettiest plants I know and a few would look delightful at the front of a mixed border— but what of the gaps left when they have been eaten? That trim kitchen-garden photographed a month later would look somewhat different. Tomatoes in early fruit are ornamental (indeed at one time they were grown only for decoration as the fruit was presumed to be poisonous), but they look ugly and top-heavy when the lower trusses have been picked and the leaves turn yellow. And what is more unkempt than potatoes ready for digging or the bare stalks of half-used Brussels sprouts?

However, having said this, I think it a pity that vegetable-growing is in decline in small gardens, if only because of the inferiority of commercial varieties. Some space might be found at least for quick-maturing saladings which must be eaten fresh, and runner-beans grown on strings on a fence are as decorative as many climbers and very productive. For greater effect the similar climbing Blue Coco bean could be grown. Its leaves have a purplish bloom, and it has violet flowers, followed by deep purple beans which turn green while they are cooking and taste delicious. An asparagus bed is quite ornamental, does not require much weeding if well-mulched, and will produce crops of this expensive delicacy for up to twenty years. The easy salads could be grown in a bed edged with pinks or thrift and backed with lavender and sage bushes.

The layout of real cottage gardens was of the simplest, with a few straight, narrow paths intersecting at right angles, and every cultivatable inch growing something. Our romanticised garden would probably have curving paths echoing in miniature the winding country lanes, and these days wider paths are needed, to accommodate a wheelbarrow, tricycle or pram. Brick or paved paths are ideal. Plain concrete and tarmac are both too stark, and gravel is difficult to control. Whatever the material, do not have more paths than you need. It looks fussy and wastes space.

The utilisation of every scrap of ground is less important today than it was to cottage-dwellers in the past, but privacy is of greater importance. A hedge is the most attractive way of ensuring this, since a wall of any height is very expensive. Some hedging which needs less attention than the ubiquitous privet was discussed in Chapter 2. At the roadside, a temporary wire fence may be necessary to save the young hedge plants from damage for a few years. Sweetbriar is another possibility. It is deciduous and will need a certain amount of pruning and training but the flowers, and more especially the scented leaves which are particularly fragrant after a shower of rain, do give extra pleasure. This is Shakespeare's eglantine. Higher hedges may be needed for a back garden, especially if there are prairie-like modern farm fields or a windswept golf-course behind. If the space can be spared, a mixed farm-type hedge could be the answer: holly and thorn, elder and hazel, elm and the spiny prunus varieties. Nuts, sloes, bullaces and elderberries would all have been welcomed as extra food by the cottager of olden times and could still be used today. For smaller plots, the most space-saving tall hedge is beech.

Fences take up less space, and no nourishment from the ground. Nothing looks more trim at the roadside than white-painted paling or 'picket-fence', but it needs regular painting and this can be a tedious job. A compromise is to have gates in this style set in a hedge, or the same kind of paling fence treated with wood preservative. Woven panels look wrong, but plain posts and rails fit in well (though children will climb and sit on them). Any low fence could have a lavender or rosemary hedge on the inside. Both are traditional and trouble-free. A high wooden fence around the back garden is often the only way to ensure privacy and to keep out, or in, children and dogs. It will not detract from the flowery profusion of the garden if it is well covered with climbers, wall-shrubs and trained fruit trees. The house walls will need similar treatment, to blend with the garden.

Espalier apples, fan-trained cherries, vines and other possibilities were discussed in Chapter 6. Strictly speaking, modern climbing roses and large-flowered clematis would not have been found in old cottage gardens, but I do not think we can exclude them, unless it be those brash bi-colour roses like Joseph's Coat. I would always give the preference to scented climbers. Two unusual ramblers to be found in the catalogues of nurseries selling old-fashioned roses are the fruit-scented yellow Gold-finch, and Veilchenblau, which has purple buds opening to a paler colour, and a fragrance like that of apples. Both, like my favourite climber, the sweetly scented, vivid pink Zéphirine Drouhin, are thornless. Sander's White resembles a scented white Dorothy Perkins. Félicité et Perpetué is a scented semi-evergreen white climbing rose which flowers rather late. Dark red Guinée and buff-yellow Gloire de Dijon are reliably frag-rant climbers and Deprez à Fleur Jaune will flood a small garden with perfume. Madame Grégoire Staechelin has sweet-pea-scented pink blooms in one splendid flowering. Emily Gray has golden buds and cream-coloured flowers, some coming after the main flush. This rose does not have much perfume, but its leaves are beautiful—richly coloured when young, shiny and evergreen to brighten up the fence all winter (at least in my sheltered garden). Fellemberg is not really a climber, but it will grow to 8ft against a fence and has sweetly scented, lilac-pink flowers opening from crimson buds. Some of these are not really old roses (Guinée, for instance, came out in 1938) but all have the old-rose look, which climbing sports of hybrid teas do not.

Honeysuckle is another 'cottagey' climber. The common wild sort (*Lonicera periclymenum*) is still the most splendidly scented, though many others have more striking flowers. Jasmine, both the winter yellow (*Jasminum nudiflorum*) and the summer white (*J. officinale*) will cover a fence, but they need a certain amount of tying in and curbing as they are sprawlers rather than climbers. *Clematis montana*, with abundant pink or white flowers, is quick-growing. The larger-flowered hybrids are much slower and need to be cut back each spring if one is not to end up with a dense cluster of flowers and foliage at the top of long bare stems. The old Everlasting Pea (*Lathyrus latifolius*) is another fence-coverer which is quick and easy to grow, and very pretty in pink or white varieties.

There are also several shrubs which, with judicious pruning, can be persuaded to mask a fence while not taking up much depth of space. Pyracantha, the evergreen firethorn with red or yellow berries, the evergreen and deciduous berberis varieties and the scented winter-sweet are three. Forsythia, a rather unsatisfactory bush when left to itself, seems to thrive on pruning and can be kept quite flat. Though no more distinguished than privet for much of the year, it has bright yellow flowers which are a welcome sight in March; and branches brought indoors even before the buds break will flower and give a foretaste of spring even in January.

(*above*) Bees on comb

(*right*) Custard and Cream,
Limnanthes douglasii,
a good bee plant

(*above*) Informal paving furnished with small plants
(*below*) Summer-house in the corner of a walled garden

An established apple or crab-apple tree is a good start for a cottage garden. If you buy one it ought really to be a standard or semi-standard, but the size of the garden must be considered, as scale is important. A pollinator may be introduced as an espalier against the fence if there is no suitable tree in the next garden. A pear or one of the less common trees mentioned in Chapter 6 would be an alternative. The ground under the tree might be grassed down. This would provide a shady place to sit, as well as making windfalls immediately visible. There is nothing worse than having to look for fallen fruit among thickly clustering plants, especially in the wasp season. A low carpeter would be an alternative to grass and bulbs could be grown with either.

Shrubs, with a few exceptions, are not traditional cottage plants. They were generally non-productive (in the practical sense), took up valuable space, and the majority remained rare and expensive for many years after their introduction from abroad. The mezereon, *Daphne mezereum*, was valued for its scented purplish-pink flowers in winter or early spring. Like *D. laureola* it was domesticated from the wild. So was that peculiar spiky plant, the Butcher's Broom (*Ruscus aculeatus*) which has the merit of thriving in dense shade, even under dripping trees, and having surprisingly bright red berries. Its common name came from its use as a kind of natural wire wool for scouring butcher's blocks and, probably, kitchen tables. Box was used for hedges, path edges and topiary, clipped into fat hens and cats with arched backs. Privet was also used for topiary but must have needed constant trimming. Witch-hazel, besides deterring witches (as did rowan) had valuable herbal properties. No doubt things like broom and guelder rose were brought into cottage gardens at times, but space was precious and there was little point if they grew wild on the nearby common. Fuchsias have been used as hedges for a very long time, and lilac is an old shrub. Perhaps the easiest thing is to go by what looks right. Flowering currants and weigela look right whereas camellias and rhododendrons do not.

G

Butcher's Broom,
Ruscus aculeatus

The shrub which must have been in most cottage gardens was the shrub rose. Cottage gardens today seem to be full of floribundas. This is understandable, since these bushes produce quantities of flowers for months on end and they can be bought neatly packaged in every hardware shop. Besides having a rigid habit, most of them are scentless and are very unlike the traditional cottage rose. The colours too are often crude. 'Brilliant brassy yellow with scarlet reverse' does not seem to me at all likely to blend with those softer harmonies which were, and are, the charm of a cottage garden.

The roses we want are not to be found in the local iron-monger's, but many of the popular catalogues list a few old roses and there are some nurseries which are growing only these. I hope they are due for a revival. Certainly the few modern roses in my garden scarcely invite a glance from visitors who often seem fascinated by the moss roses, the striped *gallica* known as Rosa Mundi or the deep pink, almost overwhelmingly fragrant *centifolias*. These are the roses we see depicted on old china, in needlework chair seats, and in the background of Victorian paintings. Some modern roses have a touch of old-world charm. Rosemary Rose, deep pink and deliciously scented, is one. Dearest, with camelli alike flowers of a bright but soft pink, and a gorgeous fragrance, is another.

The 'family history' of the old roses is confusing, to say the least of it. Anyone interested should read Graham Thomas's *Old Shrub Roses* in which the subject is patiently unravelled. There are hundreds of old roses which can never have been seen in cottage gardens, but do not let that stop you from trying them. I can mention some worthwhile representatives, but it is best to see them in flower and to make your own selection. Remember that these are shrubs and must not be pruned back to unsightly stumps. It is essential to allow them room to develop to their characteristic size and shape. They are easy-going and mix happily with all sorts of other plants.

The roses most readily associated with cottage gardens are those of the *Alba* group (which were grown in the Middle Ages), in particular Maiden's Blush, with its richly perfumed blush-pink flowers and the typical grey *alba* foliage. It grows about 5ft tall and nearly as much through. The Jacobite rose, *Alba maxima*, is a bigger bush and produces hundreds of white flowers. Celestial is a very old rose, with pretty shell-pink flowers. The *centifolias* are the old 'cabbage roses'. Of the named varieties Tour de Malakoff is the largest, up to 7ft tall, with peonylike flowers streaked with wine-red and purple—very unusual. At the other end of the scale is the seventeenth-century *Rosa centifolia pomponia*, also called De Meaux, which grows only 2ft each way and has exquisite little pink roses. Among the damask (*Damascena*) roses, Ispahan can be relied on to produce a lavish display of pink double flowers for months on end. The bush is about 5ft tall by 4ft through. The paler Blush Damask is a bigger bush and very hardy. Interesting, but less easy to grow well, is the York and Lancaster damask with some pink and some white roses on the same bush. Moss roses are *centifolias* which have developed a curious 'mossy' growth round their buds. They are sometimes depicted on Victorian china. The Old Pink Moss is as good as any, growing 4ft each way, but all are delightfully scented and altogether enchanting. Blanche Moreau has white flowers and makes a bigger bush. Even larger, and best at the back of the border, is William Lobb, the velvet moss. This has crimson flowers fading to mauve and a splendid perfume.

The *gallica* group includes the dark pink Apothecary's Rose and its pretty striped sport, Rosa Mundi. Camaieux is white, streaked with red. These grow about 4ft each way. Empress Josephine (also called *Rosa francofurtana*) is smaller, with large, clear pink flowers. The Monthly Rose of the cottage garden, so called because it flowered month after month until Christmas, is sometimes called Old Blush China. It is often seen as a bush, but will go up to about 8ft on a house wall. The majority of old roses were of various shades between white and crimson, with some mauve to purple, but yellow came in with the introduction of *Rosa foetida lutea* from Asia, one of the species roses. The Chinese *Rosa hugonis* is also yellow, and so is *Rosa xanthia* (Canary Bird), one of the earliest to flower. The species roses, the wild roses of China and Korea, are fascinating: they are the ancestors of many modern hybrids.

Then there are the Bourbons, like the Empress Josephine's Souvenir de Malmaison, and the charming sweet-scented Reine Victoria. For a difficult place, a *rugosa* rose called F. J. Grootendorst would be a good choice, for it is hardy and unfussy and has enchanting fringed petals like those of a carnation. Equally tough is the prickly Scots rose, *Rosa spinosissima* and its varieties. Indeed, old roses are so numerous and so varied that once you start, you will be continually looking for a place for just one more.

A cottage garden is not just roses. Space must be found for all those obliging old flowers which will spread and improve over the years and fill the beds to overflowing. Most will be perennials. Some may be biennials, because these will seed themselves and one can thin out or transplant their progeny as one chooses. I usually shake the seeding heads of one or two Sweet William and foxglove flowers over an odd bit of ground so that I have a supply of little plants to fill any gaps which may show up during the following spring. Seeds of hardy annuals can also be sprinkled in gaps and apart from thinning will need no further attention. Half-hardy annuals we shall probably avoid but many of these so-called bedding plants are not half-hardy at all. It is years since I bought a dozen antirrhinums in the local market but my garden has never been without snapdragons since. Mine is a mild district and the garden is sheltered (though a lamentable frost-pocket at the bottom) but even so it was a surprise to see how some antirrhinums developed into huge bushy plants and flowered year after year if the seed-pods were cut off. Some are missed, of course, and then self-sown seedlings appear in the oddest places. Wallflowers also survive for many years.

Anyone can rattle off a list of cottage-garden flowers. Canterbury bells and hollyhocks, sunflowers and pinks, Sweet William and phlox, Michaelmas daisies—but the dwarf hybrids are a recent innovation and were not in old gardens. However, they look right, as do all the simple daisylike flowers, and as they do not need to be staked, this makes them more acceptable than the tall ones. It may not be strictly correct to include modern hybrid lupins, but in moderation these mix quite happily with the others. I would exclude the huge-headed dahlias which seem to me wrong in scale and colour, the stiff, modern gladioli and the globular-headed chrysanthemums; but the older, simpler forms of these flowers fit in perfectly.

The joy of cottage plants is their 'willingness'. They are eager to grow and spread and produce flowers without much attention. This makes filling the beds to overflowing easy and inexpensive, since the plants are prepared to do their share. To start with, you might include golden rod (*Solidago*), marguerite (the old single *Chrysanthemum maximum*), and various other daisylike flowers such as perennial sunflowers, *Doronicum*, *Coreopsis*, *Rudbeckias*, and so on; delphiniums; valerian (*Centranthus*) red and white, lupins, peonies, Madonna lilies— reputed to do better in the gardens of cottages than of mansions —tiger and martagon lilies if your soil suits them, Jerusalem

Cross (*Lychnis chalcedonica*), phlox and Oriental poppy, sweet
rocket, irises and yellow flags. Bleeding Heart (*Dicentra*) is also
called Lady-in-the-Bath. (Turn a single flower upside down
and pull the sides apart to see her.) With this can be grouped
catmint and bergamot and perennial cornflowers, montbretia
(the old kinds are hardy), gypsophila, astilbes, and yellow
loosestrife. There are also aquilegias, but the old-fashioned
Granny Bonnets look better than the modern long-spurred
hybrids. If you look carefully at the dangling bells you can see
the ring of doves which gave the flower its name of columbine:
this effect is missing in the hybrids. For the front of the border
there are pinks and double daisies (*Bellis perennis*), auriculas
and primroses, Lamb's Lugs, pansies, bugle, thrift, perennial
candytuft, yellow alyssum, aubrietia and thousands more.

Columbine,
the old *Aquilegia*

It is generally the older forms of these plants which you
should look for, and anyone who has a long-established garden
will give you a barrow-load of roots to start with because they
are all plants which increase fairly quickly. This means that
they soon close up and cover the bare soil, eliminating weeding,
but they should be given room to develop into bold clumps.
Plant three pieces of root about 12in apart in a group, rather

than singly. From time to time, when the plants become so congested that the flowers are fewer, it will be necessary to lift the roots and split them up, replanting the younger outer portions and discarding the exhausted centres. Plenty of compost should be added at the same time, because thickly planted ground will obviously need feeding from time to time.

Butterflies seem to belong in a cottage garden and it is a pleasant idea to plant the flowers which attract them in a place where they can be seen from your favourite seat. The September-flowering buddleia is sometimes called Butterfly Bush, and certainly Red Admirals, Small Tortoiseshells, Peacocks and Painted Ladies can usually be seen on it. It should be cut back hard in February or March as it tends to straggle: it will still flower the same year. Late summer is the best time for these garden butterflies. Michaelmas daisies are popular, and another excellent plant is *Sedum spectabile*, sometimes called Ice Plant. Its pale green, waxy-looking foliage is decorative from spring onwards, and the flowers are present for some time before they turn pink in September and the butterflies descend on them. It grows in a neat clump about 12in high.

People often complain about the scarcity of butterflies in some areas and blame insecticides. Weedkillers are just as

Small Tortoiseshell butterfly

likely to be the cause, since Red Admirals, Peacocks and Small
Tortoiseshells are reared on stinging nettles. Eliminate the
nettles and you eliminate the butterflies. The orange and
brown Comma with jagged edges to its wings is another nettle-
feeder which has become noticeably scarcer in my lifetime.
Painted Lady caterpillars feed on thistles, hops, mallow and
occasionally nettles.

Biennials which die after flowering but seed themselves, are
useful in a cottage-type garden. Foxgloves and honesty, the
felty yellow-flowered mulleins (*Verbascum*), Evening Primrose,
the old Rose Campion (*Lychnis coronaria*) and its seldom seen
white form, Sweet William and forget-me-nots come into this
category.

Hardy annuals can also be used for gap-filling, especially
round plants which have not reached their full size, and during
the first year when all the plants will be small. One Victorian
favourite is Love-lies-Bleeding (*Amaranthus caudatus*) with long
crimson plushy tails. There is one with lime-green tails too,
much sought after by flower-arrangers. Both grow to about
2½ft if well-thinned and well-fed. This is a good annual to put
in a tub or raised bed because then its tassels do not dangle in
the mud. Against a fence you could grow annual sunflowers:
the sheer size of these and their speed of growth have a fascina-
tion, and the great round faces have a certain charm. Love-in-
a-Mist (*Nigella*) has curious seed-pods as well as pretty flowers.
The common pot marigold, annual poppies, cornflowers, clary
(*Salvia horminum*) and sweet sultan are easy and cheerful.
Nasturtiums will not only climb or trail down over a wall but
will wander along the ground and flower among other low-
growing plants.

Herbs are traditional cottage-garden plants. They may be
grown among other plants or in a bed all together. Shrubby
ones like sage and lavender and rosemary can be kept neat
with an annual trim. There are variegated and purple-leafed
sages and pink and white dwarf lavenders as well as the
common kinds. Rue, tarragon and silvery santolina make neat

clumps. Winter savory, pot marjoram and the dwarf hyssop called *Aristatus* are lower-growing. For contrast, fennel is a tall, umbelliferous plant (like cow-parsley) with feathery green or bronze foliage. It smells of aniseed. Sweet Cecily is also umbelliferous: the leaves can be used to sweeten stewed fruit with the addition of a little sugar. Woad (*Isatis tinctoria*) could be included: it was used to dye cloth as well as to paint the skin in ancient times. It is an interesting biennial with dangling seed-pods. Lemon verbena (*Lippia citriodora*) has pleasantly scented leaves, but this little bush is tender. It is worth growing it in a pot and taking it indoors in winter. Lemon balm (*Melissa officinalis*) also has lemon-scented leaves. It is a great spreader, as the mints are, but all have refreshing scents and mint julep is still something to dream about. The common one is spearmint, but there are also the bigger grey, furry applemint, Eau de Cologne mint, ginger mint, peppermint and variegated pineapple mint, all fragrant and useful. Bergamot is another spreader and so is the soapwort with pretty pale pink flowers, double or single, which is known as Bouncing Bet. This was at one time used for washing, and an extract of it is still used today for cleaning delicate antique fabrics. Tansy, once an ingredient of that peculiar Easter dish called tansy pudding, has fascinating crimped and cut bright green leaves and yellow flowers resembling petal-less daisies. It spreads all over the garden if allowed.

Once you include herbs in your cottage garden you are approaching the genuinely useful garden of long ago, and it may be hoped that you will experiment with these flavours in the kitchen. At one time they were necessary to add savour to the limited and boring diet of the poor, but it seems to me that they are even more essential to improve the frozen chickens and frozen fish which come our way today. Lemon balm in stuffing has a beneficial effect on the most negative poultry, and my first taste of chervil soup, made from the simplest ingredients, was a revelation. (Chervil is an annual which can easily be grown in a flowerpot outside the back door, as can dill, caraway, coriander, parsley and many others.) There is enormous interest to be found in tracking down suitable plants to create the picturesque effect we think of as characterising a cottage garden, but we get closer to our cottage-dwelling fore-bears if we grow the plants which were familiar to them and use them as they did. A whole range of country skills is there to be explored, and there is surprising pleasure to be had from sleeping between lavender-scented sheets, drinking a fragrant balm wine, plucking sprigs of fennel for a piquant sauce to accompany a dish of herrings, or brewing a refreshing mint tea to drink in the garden on a hot afternoon.

Chapter 8

Bee Gardens

THERE IS nothing more restful and more evocative of summer than the hum of bees in a garden, and it has always amazed me that a creature which sounds so soothing, not to say soporific, is in fact working itself to death. When honey was the only sweetener available everyone had hives in the garden, and the honey was robbed each autumn by simply killing off the bees. A few stocks would be retained through the winter and built up again the following year. Swarms of wild bees could not have been hard to find: the forests of old England must have sheltered millions of colonies living in hollow trees. In a sense, bees are still as wild as they ever were. The honey-bees murmuring over your lavender hedge may have come from a hive, but they could just as well have issued from a colony living in a wall or a tree, and neither would be any 'tamer' than the other.

Apart from the peculiar pleasure of watching them at work, encouraging bees in a garden has practical advantages. While gathering nectar to convert into honey—which is as much a manufactured article as marmalade—and the pollen necessary to feed their young, bees perform a valuable service by transferring pollen from flower to flower, a sort of artificial insemination organised by nature. Without pollination there would be no fruit, nuts or seeds. Because the fertilising pollen must come from a flower of the same kind, the bee works only one species at a time. The observant watcher in a deck-chair

119

will see that bees do not flit from apple-blossom to laburnum, from iris to cornflower, but confine their attention to one kind of flower. So the plants benefit the bees and the bees benefit the plants, and human beings benefit from both without lifting a finger.

So whether the gardener wants large, handsome rose-hips on his *Rosa rubrifolia* or splendid raspberries for Sunday dinner, he needs the services of bees, and he will *not* spray everything in his garden with the many poisonous chemicals available. It is no use spraying broad-bean plants to get rid of the blackfly when the flowers are open, because then the bees which would ensure a good crop of beans will be poisoned. The time to kill the blackfly was before the flowers appeared. Once they have, it is better to pinch out the infected tops and to forget about insecticides. *No open flowers should be sprayed.* Fruit trees should be dealt with before the buds open and a good while after the petals have fallen. Sometimes the wind will strip off the apple-blossom petals, but honey-bees will still pollinate the flowers because the important part is still there: the petals are only window-dressing. Then it is important to notice what else you may be spraying accidentally. Spray falls on to grass under fruit trees and possibly on to dandelions growing there, and dandelions are valuable plants from the bees' point of view. They open early in the year when flowers are not plentiful, and when bees are already raising young brood ready for the summer's work. Larvae need pollen, the protein food essential for growth, and dandelions are a good source. There are ways round the problem. In a small orchard the dandelions could be cut down with a grass-hook before spraying is done: there would be a fresh, uncontaminated supply a few days later. Or spraying could be done on a dull day or in the evening, when the flowers would be closed and the vital parts protected.

Bumble-bees are perhaps most noticeable in a garden. They are gentle creatures: I have never heard of anyone being stung by a bumble-bee. They are scientifically classified as *Bombus*, a name which seems peculiarly apt. Honey-bees (*Apis mellifera*) are much smaller and are often mistaken for wasps, if they are noticed at all. Bumble-bees all die in the autumn, except the fertilised queens who sleep the winter away in holes and emerge to start new colonies in the spring. Honey-bees survive as a community because they store quantities of honey to eat during the cold, dull, flowerless months, and keep warm by clustering together. A colony of bumble-bees may number 200 or 300, but at its peak there will be up to 60,000 honey-bees in a flourishing hive. Obviously the latter are of far greater value in the national economy. Their production of honey is of minor importance compared with their role as pollinators. You will see bumble-bees at work when it is too cold, wet or windy for honey-bees, but there are not enough of them to save the fruit crop if there is bad weather in blossomtime.

Bumble-bee

In a garden, bumble-bees and foxgloves seem to go together. Other plants whose nectar is available only to the longer tongues of bumble-bees are bergamot, antirrhinums, rhododendrons, columbines, convolvulus, scarlet salvias and purple buddleias, but of course bumble-bees also visit most of the flowers which honey-bees patronise.

Whether you have bumble-bees in your garden or not is a matter of chance, but you can ensure a good supply of pollinators by installing a hive of honey-bees—and you will probably get some honey, too. Beekeeping is enormously interesting and could be carried on almost anywhere, in a small way. It must be said at once that bees do need careful management, and it is only fair to your neighbours to learn how to look after them properly and to take the necessary steps to prevent their being a nuisance. I will return to this point later. Firstly, what sort of garden would be most suitable? Most of the easily maintained gardens described in this book would answer the purpose. The informal fruit garden dealt with in Chapter 6 would clearly benefit from the presence of a hive of bees. Whatever the layout, preference can be given to those shrubs, trees and flowering plants which honey-bees visit, and which anyone might include in his garden for the pleasure of watching bees at work.

Fruit trees come high on the list because many are a suitable size for modern gardens, though when they are in blossom the weather seldom invites one to sit outside watching bees. Apples blossom later than pears, plums or cherries, and the later varieties like Winston and Edward VII are likely to be in flower when warmer days arrive. From the bees' point of view, crab-apples are just as attractive, supplying nectar and pollen, but double-flowered ornamental varieties are sterile and will not be visited by bees. Almond, peach and apricot trees flower so early that the weather is often too cold for insects, and pollination must be done by hand to be satisfactory. However, if there is a hive in the same garden, the bees will work the blossom whenever there is a sunny spell because they have not far to go home if the temperature drops suddenly. Pears usually flower before apples, but where they coincide bees prefer the apple-blossom. The earliest plums to flower are the Myrobalan or cherry plum and its purple-leafed variety, and the sloe or blackthorn (*Prunus spinosa*), whose branches are often thick with white blossom in February. Both will be worked by bees if weather conditions allow. The wild cherry or gean (*Prunus avium*) and the Bird cherry (*P. padus*) are as popular as the cultivated kinds. Laurels also belong to the genus *Prunus*, though they are hardly fruit trees. The cherry laurel, *P.*

laurocerasus, flowers in April but it is visited at other times for the nectar secreted in the extra-floral nectaries on the backs of its young leaves. The Portugal Laurel (*P. lusitanica*) flowers later. This makes a most attractive small evergreen tree, grown naturally on a single trunk. Quinces and medlars are also worked by bees. These flower after the apples, and are ornamental small trees for any garden.

Many of the best trees for bees are too large for the average garden. Limes are possibly the best nectar-producers of all, but they are huge, and if they are pollarded they will not bear blossom. They also drip honey-dew, which makes the ground under them sticky and encourages the growth of an unsightly black fungus on the leaves. Sycamores pose the same problems and also spread their offspring far and wide. There are some smaller, less common limes such as *Tilia mongolica* and the free-flowering, fern-leafed lime, *T. platyphyllos Asplenifolia*. The field maple (*Acer campestre*) is an attractive tree, seldom exceeding 35ft tall. The common horse-chestnut may easily be double that, though the pink-flowered one (*carnea*) is smaller and flowers later. Where there is room for a large tree, the impressive Indian horse-chestnut (*Æsculus indica*) would be a better choice than the common sort as it does not flower until June, when there is often a dearth of nectar known as the 'June gap'. The exotic-sounding Tree of Heaven, *Ailanthus altissima*, and the Pagoda Tree, *Sophora japonica*, are both good for bees and make imposing specimens in a large garden. The stately yew is a splendid source of March pollen, but it is perhaps best left to the churchyard.

One of the best sources of early pollen is the willow. Catkins come from March onwards. Some willows are huge trees, but the goat willow or sallow (*Salix caprea*) and the grey willow (*S. cinerea*) are really shrubs and *S. daphnoides*, the violet willow, is an ornamental small tree with waxy purple shoots and large catkins. In suitable weather willows yield nectar too. The inconspicuous white flowers of the holly secrete abundant nectar and this tree is never too big for a modest garden.

Another evergreen whose unspectacular flowers attract bees is sweet bay, *Laurus nobilis*, better known as a clipped tub specimen. The young plant needs winter protection, but it will develop into a dense bush or small tree able to survive hard frost, though some of the leaves may be damaged.

Other ornamental trees of reasonable dimensions which bees visit are the Judas Tree (*Cercis siliquastrum*) with pink flowers in May, and the Indian Bean Tree (*Catalpa bignonioides*) which blooms in July or August. I have seen bees working the white flowers of the false acacia, *Robinia pseudoacacia*, in a hot summer, but the following year the flowers were ignored. This is an elegant, light-foliaged tree which can grow rather large but never massive. Its variety *Semperflorens* has some flowers all through the summer instead of a lavish display in June.

Hazel catkins offer abundant pollen as early as January, if there are bees available to collect it. Beekeepers claim that in some years good crops of honey are obtained from hawthorn but that in others the tree is never visited. This may depend on the weather or on the availability of something else, such as apple-blossom, which would be preferred. Double-flowered hawthorns are of no interest to bees.

Among shrubs, *Buddleia globosa* with balls of orange flowers is outstanding, and it helps to fill the 'June gap'. *Cotoneaster horizontalis*, with fishbone-patterned branches and tiny pink flowers, swarms with bees in May. Other cotoneasters are also visited, especially the June-flowering varieties. If there are warm days in February, bees will work the scented pink *Daphne mezereum* blossom for nectar and pollen. Gorse, *Mahonia aquifolium* and Japanese quince all flower early in the year and will attract attention on fine days. All the berberis species (several are described in Chapter 4) are valuable: they mostly flower in April and May though *Berberis wilsonae* is later. Broom yields deep orange pollen in May and June and the earlier white-flowered Portugal broom is also well worked most years. Evergreen *Escallonia*, with small pink flowers, is another source of June nectar.

A dovecot makes a striking tall feature in a cottage garden

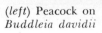

(*left*) Peacock on
Buddleia davidii

(*right*) Bumble-bee and
Buddleia globosa

The flowers of *Weigela* are actually too deep for honey-bees, but nectar is extracted through holes made near the base of the trumpet, possibly by bumble-bees. This also happens with common fuchsia which is a valuable August bee-plant. In mild districts fuchsias can reach tree-like proportions, as in Ireland, but a severe winter will kill the plant above ground. However, new shoots will spring up to 3–4ft in the following summer and flower well. A seldom-seen shrub called *Perowskia atriplicifolia*, with lavender-blue flowers, is also popular in August and September. It too is sometimes cut down in winter but it springs up again. It needs good drainage and a sunny spot to do well. The neat evergreen *Hebes*, formerly called veronicas, attract many bees. There are autumn- and summer-flowering varieties, all covered with mauve to purple, or sometimes white, spires.

Hundreds of different flowers may be worked by bees at some time or another, depending on what rival attractions are in bloom at the same time. Most of the bulb flowers—snowdrops, crocuses, scillas and narcissi—are sources of pollen for bees brave enough to venture out in the unpredictable spring weather. They will visit wallflowers and arabis and aubrietia, the hardy March-flowering *Doronicum*, forget-me-nots and honesty. In May the biennial known as Custard and Cream (*Limnanthes douglasii*) hums with bees. It makes a rewarding display because the yellow and white flowers are very abundant. The plants are only 6in tall, so they make a pleasant edging, and they drop their seed to ensure plenty of plants for the following year.

Bees visit most of the old cottage-garden flowers, though not the newer hybrids and double forms: for instance, the old daisylike pot marigolds, but not the modern ones which look like chrysanthemums. Cornflowers, campanulas, rudbeckia, achillea, single sweet rocket—all these claim attention. Poppies, from the wispy little field poppy to the Oriental, are sources of pollen, but not of nectar. Poppy pollen is nearly black and can be seen in the bees' pollen-baskets as they fly away. Pollen-spotting is a relaxing amusement on a hot day. The colour

H

varies surprisingly, from the brick red taken from horse-
chestnut flowers, through many shades of orange, yellow and
green, to slate-grey and black. Thalictrum, columbines, hypericum and single peonies are worked for pollen and hollyhocks
are a prolific source. One sometimes sees several bees revelling
in a single hollyhock flower, and flying away with their backs
covered and pollen-baskets bulging, while spilled pollen settles
on the leaves below. That curious bulbous plant, the Crown
Imperial, is visited by bees for its abundant and easily seen
nectar which is, however, rather watery. Globe thistles
(*Echinops*) are worked for nectar and so are the large thistle-like
heads of the biennial teasel.

Among annuals, bees particularly seem to like the orange
pollen from the showy Californian poppies (*Eschscholtzias*), and
the little blue and white *Nemophila*, sometimes called Baby Blue
Eyes, is also well patronised. This makes a good edging. Seed
can be sown in autumn for early flowers or in June for late
summer bloom. Mignonette will attract bees all day, and it
must be one of the most fragrant flowers. It has been said that
mignonette yields more nectar for the space it occupies than
any other plant, but I have no way of confirming this. Among
taller annuals the garden balsam, *Impatiens roylei*, is about 2ft
tall with large pale pink bells, and *Phacelia tenacetifolia*, sometimes called wild heliotrope, grows to about 18in and has
lavender-blue flowers. Both are very attractive to bees.

Many bee-plants are purplish-blue in colour. The perennial
June-flowering *Salvia superba* is one which merits a place in any
garden. It grows 2–3ft high, likes sunshine, and flowers for a
long time. Of similar size is *Veronica spicata* with pink and white
as well as purple forms. Catmint (*Nepeta mussinii*) is more
sprawling than these two. It is sometimes recommended for the
front of the border, but it will cover the path if it is planted too
near the edge. Incidentally, this is *not* the catnip irresistible to
cats: that is *Nepeta cataria*, a wild plant with pink-dotted white
flowers, which is also a good bee-plant. The famous American
apiarist Moses Quinby is supposed to have said that it was the

only flower he would plant in quantity to increase honey-production. Later in the year the bees will be busy with the Michaelmas daisies and golden rod and the simpler sorts of dahlia. They also share the butterflies' enthusiasm for *Sedum spectabile*, the Ice Plant, with its flat pink inflorescences and waxy foliage.

Many herbs have flowers in the attractive blue-to-purple colour range: mint and lavender, sage, thyme, rosemary and hyssop. Not for nothing did the cottager of olden times have his hives in the herb garden. Herbs can be grown in a special bed but they will also fit in anywhere in the garden. Lavender and rosemary can be used for low hedging. Creeping thyme will grow between paving stones, or carpet a bank you do not want to mow. Basil, borage, summer and winter savory and many other culinary herbs will attract their quota of bees. Melilot (also called sweet clover) is regarded as a herb, though it is hard to visualise it in a neat, formal herb-garden. Despite its name it does not resemble clover at all, being about 4ft high with racemes of white or yellow blossoms. The name means *mel* (honey) and *lotus* (a flower), and bees work it eagerly, but it is an awkward garden plant. Possibly it would be best grown against a sunny fence, and tied up to it. It is in fact perennial but is usually treated as a biennial.

The kitchen-garden is of little interest to bees as most vegetables are harvested before they flower. Where onions, leeks, celery, parsnips and such things run to seed, bees work the blossom, as they do where these crops are grown on a large scale for seed-production. All garden beans benefit from the attentions of bees. I have seen them working the bell-shaped flowers of asparagus when it has run to fern. In the fruit garden they are always active. Strawberries are little favoured but blackberries, raspberries, logans and all sorts of currants attract attention, and good crops are ensured if bees are plentiful and the weather allows them to work.

Among climbers, honeysuckle is not of much use to honeybees, despite its name. Pollen is collected from clematis, and the self-clinging *Hydrangea petiolaris* is visited by bees, but I have never seen them on other hydrangeas which are mainly composed of sterile florets. Virginia creeper (*Parthenocissus quinque-folia*) swarms with bees collecting both nectar and pollen when its inconspicuous flowers are open: one would hardly notice the flowers if it were not for the bees. However, this climber is too rampant for most modern houses, though it can be used to drape a dead tree or a tall ugly outbuilding. Ivy is a useful climber. The peculiar greenish flowers do not appear until late autumn, but are often humming with bees on mild November days. The nectar is freely produced and very concentrated, and would seem to be ideal for filling spare corners in the storage combs before really severe weather sets in.

From this it will be seen that a pleasant garden could be planned using mainly those plants which attract bees. The chief requirement is that the garden should be sunny. Most bee-plants do better with sun; and bees prefer to work flowers which are in the sun, ignoring similar ones in shade. This may have some connection with the relative levels of nectar. The chosen plants should be arranged in large clumps of the same kind, not dotted about singly, so that the bees will find them and think them worth attention. Bold groups of plants are always more effective anyway, and make for a stronger, less fussy, design. Another point to bear in mind is the placing of the bee-plants in relation to paths. Bees seldom sting when they are away from their hive but many people are afraid of them. It is not wise to have a shrub swarming with them so close to a path that visitors must brush against it to reach the door. Avoid putting bee-plants around doors and under windows which are often kept open, and do not grow creeping thyme in paving or paths you want to walk on.

It is a short step from filling your garden with bee-plants to deciding that your own bees might as well benefit from them. There is the lure of honey, of course, but also the bees themselves are of extraordinary interest. The queen is the head of the hive, the mother of every bee in it, but she is in no sense a ruler. She secretes something called 'queen substance', which the workers who constantly feed and groom her obtain from her. It could be likened to a drug which keeps them happy. If they do not get enough, either because there are too many workers or because the queen is failing, they replace her. It is an automatic response to the lack of their 'happiness drug', not a conscious decision. They raise a new queen, and if the hive is overcrowded the old queen leaves with a number of other bees (a swarm) to start a new colony elsewhere. An aged or sick queen would probably remain until she died, even when the young one took over her job. This is simply to lay eggs, 2,000 or more a day.

Honey-bees: queen, drone and worker

The queen is not a reigning monarch—indeed, she is very unadaptable and limited—but she has a regal look. 'The Queen bee is a fair and statelie creature . . .' wrote John Gedde (1721) in *The English Apiary*, and he was right. Most potential beekeepers get a thrill the first time they see a queen on the comb. I remember the feeling. You look for her half idly, not really believing you will be able to pick out *one* bee among so many, though you know there are certain differences . . . and suddenly, there she is, quite unmistakable, moving with slow dignity across the patterned comb. As she passes them the young bees who are not yet foragers turn to face her. They groom her and feed her if she wants food. You watch her move on, and other bees turn towards her. The queen has a quality which can only be described as charisma.

The other occupants of the hive are about 1,000 drones (the necessary but idle males), and 40–50,000 workers (sexually undeveloped females) who toil all their lives. They make wax within their bodies and build the marvellous assemblage of symmetrical cells which is honeycomb. No storage system more efficient and more economical of materials could be devised. The beekeeper provides flat sheets of wax foundation to persuade the bees to build their combs inside movable light wooden frames. In the hives I use, each comb contains 9,000 perfectly hexagonal cells. The workers clean out the cells, feed the larvae, repair comb, guard the entrance, carry out the dead and stop up cracks with propolis, a brownish resin collected from trees. If the hive gets too hot in summer, over 95°F, they can cool it by fanning with their wings. In extreme cases they carry in water and spray it over the combs so that the fanning will evaporate it and bring down the temperature. Lastly, they become foragers, leaving the dark hive for the sunny brilliance of the garden to collect pollen and nectar. Honey is a concentrated product, and roughly 3lb of nectar must be carried in to make 1lb of honey. When conditions are right, the workers fly ceaselessly back and forth from dawn to dusk fetching their loads which seem to us so tiny. It is almost incredible that they can store enough for their own winter needs, let alone lay in a surplus which the beekeeper takes for himself. This may be 80lb from a single hive in a good year, though it is often much less. Small wonder that a bee's life is short! A worker born in spring or summer has a life expectation of only six weeks, though most autumn-born bees will live through the winter.

Obviously it would be a good idea to learn something about bees before starting to keep them. Be wary of the elderly person who offers to 'put you in the way of it', saying that there is nothing to it. In the past, many people kept bees by doing little or nothing about them, letting swarms fly off to settle in the roofs of other people's houses, and being content with what would seem by modern standards a pitifully small honey-crop. You *may* come across an ancient beekeeping genius, but it is rather unlikely. Knowledge about beekeeping, as about everything else, has increased over the years, and new equipment and easier ways of doing things have been evolved. The best plan is to join your nearest Beekeepers Association. Details can be obtained from the General Secretary of the British Beekeepers Association, whose address is given in the Appendix. Through the local Association you will be able to visit apiaries and meet beekeepers, and decide whether you really want to keep bees and what equipment you will need if so. There are often benefits by way of bulk orders of honey-jars etc, and the Association will also know what evening classes or courses of instruction are available in your district. The more you learn about bees the more fascinating you will find them. They are never completely predictable. A swarm of bees is supposed to hang like a ball on the branch of a tree, so that a skep or cardboard carton can be put underneath, and a thump on the branch will cause the whole thing to drop into the container like a ripe fruit. But the first swarm you see will inevitably be wrapped around a telegraph pole or else be in the middle of a thick and thorny hedge. Beekeeping demands sharp wits, or at least a degree of native cunning.

If you imagine a beehive like a neat, white-painted 'chalet'

standing beneath the apple tree on the lawn, put the picture
out of your mind. This old-fashioned type of hive has nothing
to commend it except superficial prettiness, and the chances
are that the best place for your hive will not be where you
would want to have a garden ornament anyway. The most
popular British hive is the National; but the most widely used
hive in the world is the Langstroth. This is the one I use, or
rather, the improved version of it developed at the Hampshire
College of Agriculture and known as the New Standard hive.
It is very satisfactory and easy to manage.

But to return to the subject of plants. Every expert will tell
you that whatever you plant in your garden, it will not affect
the amount of honey you get. I have read that an acre of
raspberries or forty mature lime trees in the area would be
required to increase the honey yield by a noticeable amount.
This may be so. But I do feel that sources of nectar and pollen
close to the hive can make all the difference to a colony's
chances of survival in bad weather, and will therefore ultimately
affect the honey-crop. When it is cold or showery, bees will
not fly far from the hive because if they get wet or chilled they
will never reach home again. They will not risk going to a
field of sainfoin two miles away, but they will be quite prepared
to visit the *Buddleia globosa* and the cornflowers at the end of
the garden. This is particularly so early in the year when
brood-rearing begins and a supply of pollen is vital. Weather
is unreliable, and bees with access to a couple of catkin-covered
willows close at hand are certainly better off than those with
nothing. It is not in the honey-flows but in the lean times that
bees will benefit from garden flowers, so the most valuable
plants will tend to be those which bloom very early, or during
the 'June gap', or late in the year.

A suitable spot for a beehive can be found in most established
gardens, but the following points should be considered if you
are planning from scratch. The hive should be on high ground
rather than in a hollow which will probably be a frost-pocket.
It needs shelter from the prevailing wind, and some shade from

the sun at midday. The entrance should face between south-east and south-west; probably if it looks to the east the morning sun will encourage the bees to start work early. There must be room to move all round the hive when you are opening it. The bees' flight-path to and from the entrance should be free of obstructions and should not lie across a drive or a much used path. If this is unavoidable, a screen of woven panels or a hedge 3–5yd from the front of the hive will cause the bees to rise and so pass over the heads of people using the path. Do not put the hive in a place where frequent cultivation is necessary, such as in a kitchen-garden. An orchard or the edge of a shrubbery where the bees will be relatively undisturbed is better.

Some people are afraid of bees, and neighbours are apt to look on hives with misgiving, so it is up to the beekeeper to see that his bees are not a nuisance. Improved garden crops and an occasional pot of honey will go at least some way towards reconciliation.

Chapter 9

Man-made Features

MAN-MADE FEATURES in a garden can be used to bring a dull corner to life, to underline a theme, to provide an interesting accent or contrast, or to carry the eye along a vista. Too many ornamental details cancel each other out, and create a fussy effect. We have all seen gardens where concrete gnomes peer from every bush, plastic herons dominate the pond, stone rabbits squat on the rockery and a miniature windmill whirls its sails endlessly on the lawn. One bold, well-designed decorative accent is worth all of them. It is the difference between a woman wearing a simple dress with one striking piece of jewellery and another who is hung about with a variety of little brooches and bangles and necklets and earrings. Restraint should be the keynote.

Sculpture is purely ornamental, but many functional elements in the garden from paths to sheds may be made into decorative features. They may also be played down so as not to distract attention from something else. A white-painted cast-iron Victorian garden-seat is a very decorative object, irrespective of its use, and one would make a distinctive feature in a small garden. Three of them at intervals would be a mistake, because they would draw the eye in three different directions at once. It would be better if two of them were placed near each other on a lawn or paved area, and the third used as the sole ornament in the front garden or put in an alcove among shrubs at the end of a path, out of sight of the others. It may be argued that a seat by the pond is also needed, and one at the sunny end behind the fruit trees. This is quite reasonable, but something pleasantly unobtrusive would be as good to sit on and less distracting to the eye. A plain wooden bench would be ideal among the apple trees, and something to suit the pond should not be hard to devise.

I like plenty of seats in a garden but they need not all look like seats. If they do, the effect will be rather like that of a public park. There are certain places where people linger because there is something attractive to look at, like butterflies basking on buddleias; or because it is sheltered and catches the sun. These are the spots for seats. True, you can fetch a folding chair, but often you won't, and a relaxing and refreshing five minutes will be lost.

For a woodland or 'natural' kind of garden, a stout length of tree-trunk makes a good seat. If large, it may be let into the ground a little to prevent it from rolling: slimmer trunks can be given chocks. A simple bench can be made using tree-trunk legs and a plank, or all sawn timber. Either would be at home in this setting, though more elaborate 'rustic' seats fit better in a cottage garden. It is noticeable that people often sit on steps, so a couple of stone flags let into a sunny bank will make a good perching place, as will a coping on top of a retaining wall or double walls. At Sissinghurst Castle in Kent there is a stone seat cushioned with growing thyme: this would be pleasant enough to sit on in dry weather when it was not in flower and covered with bees. It is actually a rectangular raised bed or trough planted with creeping thyme. Something similar might be fun in a herb garden. Simple seats of no very definite style can be made by building two brick pillars and laying a single plank or slatted wooden top across them. Use $1\frac{1}{4}$in timber or thicker: flimsy woodwork looks cheap. Fillets of wood underneath at back and front will prevent the top from sliding off. Stone could also be used, perhaps in association with a stone-edged pool, or—in a modern setting—openwork concrete blocks. Such a seat built on paving close to the house might have its woodwork painted to match window-frames and doors. Study the surroundings before deciding what would look best. A formal seat intended as a focal point at the end of a straight path could be enhanced by giving it a rectangular surround of gravel or paving similar to the path, perhaps with a step up, and a background of clipped evergreens. A less formal seat surrounded with crazy paving could be backed with lavender and rosemary on top of a dry-stone wall. Leave room for the bushes to develop: lavender bushes put in at 12in high and 12in apart will make a solid hedge 4ft high *and wide* in a surprisingly short time, though there are several dwarf varieties. If you are constructing a seat you might consider making a table to match, or two little side pedestals. There are attractive though unsociable seats which encircle a tree and make a striking feature, though the tree needs to be a large one. A very informal version of the same idea can be made by building a dry-stone or mortared wall about 14in high, surrounding a tree at a little distance, with the space between filled with earth and topped with short grass or thyme.

Paths and paving can also be treated as decorative features or kept more subdued. In a garden which is full of colourful plants, an ornamental groundwork would be too much. In a room most of us would find differently patterned floor-covering, walls, curtains, and upholstery unendurable, especially since the disposition of furniture, lamps and ornaments itself creates a pattern. In a garden too, some calm areas are essential. Middle Eastern gardens are often paved with very decorative patterned tiles, but these are associated with pale walls, green foliage, and water in pools and channels, all of which are restful elements. Grey or buff stone (real or imitation) or mellow brick blends with flowers rather than vying with them, but multicoloured slabs or a patterned paving of different materials used together will have a fussy effect unless they are contrasted with plain grass or mainly evergreen shrubs. Paths are sometimes made of very unusual materials. I have seen 'stepping-stones' made from circular slices cut from a tree-trunk, but these need to be soaked in preservative and they will still grow moss if laid in the sort of shady woodland conditions where they would look most at home. Another possibility is a pine-needle path which is pleasant and springy to walk on. There must be a rubble base to ensure good drainage, then at least a 4in depth of pine-needles on top, confined at the edges to prevent it from scattering. I have not made one myself and am inclined to wonder whether the birds would throw it about while looking for insects under the needles, but it is an interesting idea, especially in a conifer garden.

On the whole, the material used for paths and paving should make a background for the plants; but in a small town garden it may be the principal decorative feature, since colour is usually limited under such conditions and the main contrast to the hard surfaces is most likely to be the varying greens of foliage. All sorts of interesting effects can be devised, from an arrangement of different materials in random rectangles (bricks and slabs and tiles, brushed concrete and cobbles) to a chessboard of alternate stones and granite setts. It is also possible to incorporate a decorative motif, such as a compass rose picked out with small bricks or pebbles. Designs of this sort ought to be strong and simple, and they are more interesting if they have some relevance either to the owner or to the history of the house itself. Personal mementoes can be great fun—panels of concrete decorated with pebble mosaics by members of the family, or with a design to commemorate a national or family event. I often wonder who made certain souvenirs of past owners which exist in my garden, and enjoy the thought of leaving something behind for future occupants to speculate about. One man I know had slabs of cement impressed with the baby footprints of his children laid in his terrace, but he lifted them and took them to several homes. Cat and dog footprints are usually obtained unintentionally.

Steps may be a decorative, as well as a practical, feature, but they should above all be safe. A loose brick or a tilting slab can be very dangerous. Treads should be broad enough to take the largest foot in comfort: a 9in brick is not really adequate. Wide shallow steps are the ideal: a steep narrow flight can look as mean as a tenement staircase. Where lawn is on two levels, spacious grass-treads with brick risers look attractive, especially if round-nosed bricks are used for the top of the riser. As the strips of grass are contained in brick at both edges they are no problem to mow, especially if one uses an air-cushioned mower, or one of the little mains electric ones. Thyme, camomile or pennyroyal would need less attention than grass but should not be allowed to flower. Steps associated with a terrace should be planned to blend with it. They can be given greater importance if they are constructed so that the lower steps extend round three sides of the one above; or if they widen as they descend; or are dignified with side walls and pillars or urns flanking the bottom step. Steps can also be fitted neatly into a corner. Even cottage-garden steps can be emphasised by means of ordinary flowerpots filled with nasturtiums or pelargoniums standing at the sides, providing there is plenty of room to walk. Brick and stone steps leading into lawn should have an extra tread at the bottom, flush with the grass, to simplify mowing. This may be extended into a rectangle or semicircle of paving.

A piece of sculpture or an ornament such as a sundial, bird-bath or dovecot can make a tremendous difference to a garden if it is good of its kind and cleverly sited. There are deformed-looking concrete cherubs which are not an asset anywhere. Other modern reproductions are distinguished and they blend well with the garden after a few months' exposure to the elements. It is surprising how few pieces of contemporary sculpture are seen in the gardens of modern houses, considering their obvious affinity with present-day architecture. I have often thought how much I would enjoy having one of Barbara Hepworth's hollow, egg-shaped forms in my garden; and how much my small boy would love climbing through it! Few people can afford an objet d'art of this magnificence, but there must be interesting work done by Art College students which would be suitable, and might even appreciate in value.

A small piece could always be given prominence by being mounted on a pillar or pedestal of some sort. For period gardens, ornaments can sometimes be bought when old houses are demolished, but they are often costly. Surprising things can be found in Council yards or those of demolition and salvage firms. I have seen, for instance, splendid old chimneypots with raised decoration: one of these would make an unusual sundial or it could be filled with earth and trailing plants to make a tall accent.

The 'statuary' of the cottage garden was topiary. This ancient art was practised by the Romans, but it was probably at the height of its popularity in Tudor times and, later, when Dutch gardens became the rage in the reign of William and Mary. Sets of massive chessmen in clipped yew covering half an acre may still be seen in the grounds of some stately homes. At the other end of the scale are the jaunty cocks, fat teapots and graceful dolphins which the cottager amused himself by shaping out of box. The front garden of a bungalow near my home contains a privet settee and two armchairs which shows that the art is not dead, though I find it difficult to admire this particular manifestation. However, I do not share Francis Bacon's opinion of 'images cut in juniper and other garden stuff': he thought them childish. In an unsophisticated cottage garden a clipped bird or animal is a far more appropriate decoration than a half-clad nymph or concrete gnome, and real skill is needed to make a good shape. In its simplest form, topiary means clipped cones and spheres, tapered spirals and domes, which are really only formalised natural plant-forms. Close to the house, on a terrace or flanking a doorway or steps, a pair of clipped bushes is a valuable link between architectural and natural elements and can also be used to frame a more distant feature. A clipped spiral or obelisk may be just the tall accent needed to relieve a flat area. Since topiary can look rather odd in the growing stages, there is something to be said for having the bush in a pot which can be moved into a vantage point when it has become fit to be seen.

Most people could build a simple sundial. Given a suitable piece of stone, many could chip out an interesting abstract shape or a primitive human form. One of the truest old sayings is the one about never knowing what you can do until you try. A modern brick sundial is shown in the drawing. This would be more in keeping with a house built of similar bricks than would an antique one in cast stone, but made from old bricks it would look equally well in a cottage garden. Dials are still being made today. The informal stone column could be made from crazy-paving left-overs with a dial, pot or figure on top. A round brick tub can be built in any place where a large urn or other container would be appropriate, such as the end of the

Brick sundial to make

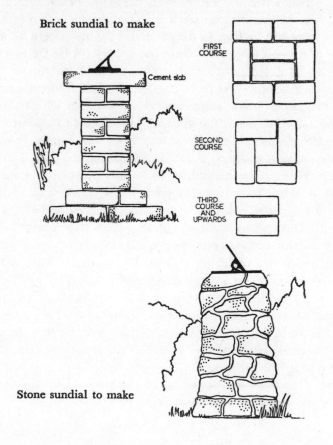

FIRST COURSE

SECOND COURSE

THIRD COURSE AND UPWARDS

Cement slab

Stone sundial to make

(*right*) A small,
easily-managed
garden
(*below*) Informal
cottage-style
planting

Playhouse converted from outdoor 'privy'

T-junction for turning in a front garden. Try to work out your own design using the materials at hand, and do not attempt anything too elaborate.

For a tall feature, any pleasantly shaped container could be given a base of the required height and filled with plants whose flowers dangle and are not seen to their best advantage at knee-level. Fuchsias are particularly good; and so is the annual, Love-lies-Bleeding, whose red or green plushy tassels often get muddy when the plant is grown in a border. Eighteenth-century urns have a rather tall, narrow shape: Victorian ones are much wider and shallower. An elderly woman I knew had two of the latter, very large ones, on paving at the back of her house. The rest of her garden was given up to shrubs, and grass which a neighbour cut once a month. The stone containers gave her manageable flower-beds which she could get round easily and tend without stooping, and they were within easy reach of the kitchen-tap for watering. This is an idea worth considering for an invalid. Some department-store annuals or a packet of mixed seed would ensure a colourful summer display, but dwarf shrubs, small bulbs and winter-flowering heathers would provide year-round interest. Herbs and salads are another possibility. There are some simple modern bowls, made of asbestos cement, which could be used in the same way, raised on a low platform of concrete blocks if necessary; or a circular, raised bed could be built of bricks. In various muni-cipal schemes I have seen straight-sided concrete plant-containers which bear a marked resemblance to the pre-cast concrete rings which are used for lining large man-holes, and which may in fact be one and the same. These can be stacked to the required height. Local authorities favour a rather austere style of planting, but these simple containers look best filled to overflowing, and with trailers softening the hard line of the rim. The concrete can be coloured with cement paint if appropriate.

A dovecot is an effective garden feature only if it contains doves. Any enthusiast will tell you what sort of accommodation is necessary for the birds' comfort, but I have seen a traditional white-painted dovecot and a thatched one in different gardens, and also a very modern arrangement of various sized boxes on squared posts of different lengths which, from a distance, had the look of an abstract sculpture.

Sheds and summer-houses are more often eyesores than decorative garden features. They are too large to be inconspicuous so, if one must have them at all, they may as well look as attractive as possible. A tool-shed is best built as part of the house or garage, so that equipment is handy and there is no need for a shack in the garden. In these days of central heating, a redundant coal-shed attached to the back of the house might be converted for this purpose. A cupboard under the stairs, provided with an outside door instead of an inside one, would be large enough to accommodate all the tools needed for a small modern garden, and might be considered by anyone having a house built.

It is questionable whether a summer-house is an asset in a small garden, which often has the enclosed and intimate atmosphere of a room. Few summer-houses rotate so that one can be sure of getting sun without wind; and one can almost always find a pleasanter spot in which to sit, according to prevailing conditions. Too often the summer-house degenerates into a storage place for rubbish. However, it must be admitted that an attractive small building can be a delightful garden feature, as eighteenth-century designers realised. What is more picturesque than the romantic ruin seen through the artfully contrived gap in the wild garden, or the little classical temple reflected in the lake? Unfortunately, this effect can hardly be reproduced in our suburban one-twelfth of an acre.

All the same, the idea of a 'folly' is an attractive one, and it would offer scope for ingenuity in constructing something more decorative than a hut of cedar sectional in which to house the mower. In a woodland garden a rustic shelter or arbour with a bench in it would make a fitting end to a path and tax no one's skill at carpentry. Climbers trained over a framework of rough timber would suit the surroundings. A Georgian type of house might be echoed in a formal little brick building with a flat roof and stone balls along the parapet. Proportions of door, windows and glazing bars need care, and woodwork should probably be painted white. At the least it would make an attractive storage place for tools and step-ladders and the sort of garden furniture which must not be left outside; and it would be useful where there is a terrace at the far end of the garden. Not at all weather-proof but extremely decorative are the white wrought-iron 'birdcages' seen in Regency gardens and covered with a large-leafed climber for summer shade. The usual ogee roof would be difficult to reproduce, but something similar in white-painted trellis could be evolved to suit almost any garden. Many dwellings are of no particular style, so this leaves a wider field for an imaginative person to dream up an attractive little garden building which does not conflict. Obviously a thatched hut with bark walls would be inappropriate, unless it were out of sight of the house in a woodland glade. Sometimes an existing building can be altered to make a charming feature. I have seen old stables, with the front wall replaced by timber pillars and beams, converted into a delightful loggia for summer meals.

Children love little houses, which brings me to the small building shown on page 144, and to the subject of gardens for children. My home was originally three cottages, and this building was one of the outside privies. It was high for its floor area and light was admitted only through a 10in gap between the top of the door and its frame. Inside was a brick floor, a wooden seat and a bucket. I dismantled the roof, took seven courses of bricks from the walls, made a window-opening and then reconstructed the roof with some new beams and battens. The existing door was cut to fit a reduced doorway, and a casement-window was made and glazed with 2in mesh Claritex which is safer than glass and gives a leaded-light effect. The repointing of the walls was not finished at the time the photograph was taken. The building is of the same materials as the big house, with no whimsical touches, and it blends happily with its surroundings. It is weather-proof, so it makes a handy shelter from summer showers and is furnished with a table and stools for tea-parties. The little hedge of lonicera, berberis and yellow privet (cuttings from around the garden) hides the worst untidiness, gives greater privacy, and is clipped by the seven-year-old owner himself when the spirit moves him.

The sand-pit is 4½ft square and made from second-hand 2in-by-9in boards, with old tiles laid loose on ashes in the bottom to provide drainage. Half a yard of washed builders' sand, with a collection of buckets and spades, patty-pans and wooden spoons completed this valuable plaything. Many of the things which children enjoy playing with are not very aesthetic, but a spot partially screened from the house and furnished with old barrels and oil-drums, boxes and planks and large-diameter drain-pipes will earn you hours of peace. A pensioned-off car is a glory to an older child, but remove the battery, and the petrol tank too, or at least wash it out and leave the cap off to eliminate dangerous fumes. Prop it on *wooden* blocks, if you must, as concrete ones and bricks are apt to split suddenly. An old bedspring on blocks makes a good trampolin for children whose feet are large enough not to get stuck in the mesh. A plank-and-log seesaw is not unattractive: developers cut down many trees, so trunks can sometimes be acquired before they burn them. A really big one is good for clambering on, or transforming into a castle, ship or dinosaur, as well as being an asset in a woodland setting. Climbing-frames are expensive and often ugly, but an existing tree can some-times be adapted by carefully removing one or two branches, adding beams across those remaining (securely fastened), and providing a means of getting up the first awkward bit. A swing is easier on the eye if hung from a branch rather than from a scaffolding-type frame, and it can later be joined by a rope-ladder. One type of swing is a single rope secured through a circular seat of thick plywood which will not split. Whatever ropework is provided should be frequently checked for wear

and rotting, especially if it is left out in the winter. Car tyres
hung on a rope are popular with some children, but the black
comes off unless the rubber is wrapped with canvas. Never
put a climbing-frame, or anything from which a child can fall,
on a paved area. Children may get dirty falling on to grass but
they are unlikely to break their necks or knock their front
teeth out. Incidentally, many a broken tooth results from a
child getting in the way of a swing seat. A strip of rubber along
the edge might soften the blow.

I have doubts about pools for children to play in as every
year a few are drowned, often in 2in or 3in of water. A wire-
mesh cover secured in place except when there is supervision
might be the answer. A raised pool with a low parapet would
be safer for sailing boats or for paddling in than one at ground-
level, but the blow-up paddling pool is probably the safest of
all, as well as being the easiest to keep clean; and it has no hard
edges for a toddler to bang his head on. A half-barrel or
washing-up bowl filled with water will amuse a child for hours
in warm weather.

Child-oriented features can be incorporated into a good
basic layout which will remain attractive after these have been
removed or superseded. A sand-pit with a brick wall and coping
round it might be converted into a lily-pond later or, given a
floor of gravel, it could contain a built-in or portable barbecue,
with the parapet making useful seating. My son's playhouse
may become a storage place for a few years, but it will never
look unsightly and it can return to service when there is a new
generation of children.

I have emphasised the need to suit man-made features to
surroundings, but I must admit that the thoroughly eccentric
or peculiar choice can be a huge success. Some people have
this sort of flair. A woodland glade might be adorned, not with
a suitable rustic arbour, but with the kind of brightly painted
pavilion seen in paintings of medieval tournaments, and it
could be unexpectedly and romantically right. One might
bring into one's cottage garden a wooden ostrich from a

roundabout and it could look odd but delightful, or else garish, vulgar and silly. There are no rules for this sort of thing: trial and error must have the last word. But do not be afraid to try something unusual. Some extraordinary object discovered in a junk-yard might be the starting point for your whole garden plan, and very personal and distinctive the result should be. In the last analysis it is differences rather than similarities which make people interesting; and it is the expression of the owner's individuality which makes a garden interesting.

Appendix

Common Names and Their Botanical Equivalents

Alecost	Tenacetum balsamita
Almond	Prunus amygdalus
American Sweet Gum	Liquidambar styraciflua
Ash	Fraxinus
Auricula	Primula
Autumn crocus	Colchicum
Baby Blue Eyes	Nemophila
Balm	Melissa officinalis
Balsam	Impatiens roylei
Bay	Laurus nobilis
Beech	Fagus
Bergamot	Monarda didyma
Bilberry	Vaccinium myrtillus
Birch	Betula
Bird cherry	Prunus padus
Bleeding Heart	Dicentra spectabilis
Blueberry	Vaccinium corymbosum
Blue spruce	Picea pungens glauca
Bouncing Bet	Saponaria officinalis
Box	Buxus sempervirens
Broom	Cytisus
Bugle	Ajuga
Butcher's Broom	Ruscus aculeatus
Butterfly Bush	Buddleia davidii
Californian poppy	Eschscholtzia
Camomile	Anthemis nobilis
Candytuft	Iberis
Caraway	Carum carvi
Catmint	Nepeta mussinii
Catnip	Nepeta cataria

Cherry laurel	Prunus laurocerasus
Chervil	Anthriscus cerefolium
Clary	Salvia
Columbine	Aquilegia
Corkscrew hazel	Corylus avellana contorta
Cornflower	Centaurea
Costmary	Tenacetum balsamita
Cotton lavender	Santolina
Cowslip	Primula veris
Crab-apple	Malus
Cranberry	Vaccinium macrocarpum
Creeping Jenny	Lysimachia nummularia
Creeping thyme	Thymus serpyllum
Crown Imperial	Fritillaria imperialis
Custard and Cream	Limnanthes douglasii
Daffodil	Narcissus
Day-lily	Hemerocallis
Dead-nettle	Lamium
Dill	Anethum graveolens
Dogwood	Cornus
Eglantine	Rosa rubiginosa
Elder	Sambucus nigra
Elecampane	Inula helenium
Elephant's Ears	Bergenia
Elm	Ulmus
Evening Primrose	Œnothera biennis
Everlasting Pea	Lathyrus latifolius
False acacia	Robinia pseudoacacia
Fennel	Foeniculum vulgare
Field maple	Acer campestre
Fig	Ficus
Filbert	Corylus
Flag, yellow	Iris pseudacorus
Flowering currant	Ribes
Foxglove	Digitalis
Gardener's Garters	Phalaris arundinacea picta
Gean	Prunus avium
Giant hemlock	Heracleum mantegazzianum
Giant thistle	Onopordon arabicum

Goat willow	Salix caprea
Gold dust	Alyssum saxatile
Golden rod	Solidago
Gorse	Ulex europaeus
Granny Bonnets	Aquilegia
Grape hyacinth	Muscari
Grape vine	Vitis
Great Golden Knapweed	Centaurea macrocephala
Guelder rose	Viburnum opulus
Handkerchief Tree	Davidia involucrata
Hart's Tongue fern	Phyllitis scolopendrium
Hawthorn	Crataegus
Hazel	Corylus
Heather	Erica or Calluna
Holly	Ilex aquifolium
Hollyhock	Althea
Honesty	Lunaria biennis
Honeysuckle	Lonicera
Hoop Petticoat daffodil	Bulbocodium conspicuus
Hornbeam	Carpinus betulus
Horse-chestnut	Æsculus hippocastanum
Houseleek	Sempervivum
Ice Plant	Sedum spectabile
Indian Bean Tree	Catalpa bignonioides
Indian horse-chestnut	Æsculus indica
Ivy	Hedera
Japanese quince	Chaenomeles
Japonica	Chaenomeles
Jerusalem Cross	Lychnis chalcedonica
Judas Tree	Cercis siliquastrum
Lady fern	Athyrium filix-femina
Lady-in-the-Bath	Dicentra spectabilis
Lamb's Lugs	Stachys lanata
Laurel	Prunus
Laurustinus	Viburnum tinus
Lavender	Lavandula
Lawson's cypress	Chamaecyparis lawsoniana
Lemon balm	Melissa officinalis
Lemon verbena	Lippia citriodora

Lent lily	Narcissus pseudonarcissus
Lilac	Syringa
Lily-of-the-valley	Convallaria majalis
Lime tree	Tilia
London Pride	Saxifraga urbium
Loosestrife, yellow	Lysimachia punctata
Lovage	Levisticum officinalis
Love-in-a-Mist	Nigella damascena
Love-lies-Bleeding	Amaranthus caudatus
Maidenhair Tree	Ginkgo biloba
Male fern	Dryopteris filix-mas
Mallow	Malva
Maple	Acer
Marguerite	Chrysanthemum maximum
Marigold	Calendula
Marjoram	Origanum
May	Crataegus
Mazzard	Prunus avium
Medlar	Mespilus germanica
Michaelmas daisy	Aster
Mignonette	Reseda odorata
Mint	Mentha
Mock Orange Blossom	Philadelphus
Monkey-puzzle	Araucaria imbricata
Mulberry (black)	Morus nigra
Mullein	Verbascum
Myrobalan plum	Prunus cerasifera
Naked Lady	Colchicum
Nasturtium	Tropaeolum majus
Night-scented stock	Matthiola bicornis
Oak	Quercus
Old Man's Beard	Clematis vitalba
Orange-peel clematis	Clematis orientalis
Oregon Grape	Mahonia aquifolium
Pagoda Tree	Sophora japonica
Pampas grass	Cortaderia
Pansy	Viola
Parsley fern	Cryptogramma crispa
Passion-flower	Passiflora caerulea

Peach	Prunus persica
Pennyroyal	Mentha pulegium
Periwinkle	Vinca
Pink	Dianthus
Plume poppy	Macleaya cordata
Poppy	Papaver
Portugal laurel	Prunus lusitanica
Primrose	Primula vulgaris
Privet	Ligustrum
Quickset	Crataegus
Quince	Cydonia oblonga
Reed mace	Typha latifolia
Rhubarb, ornamental	Rheum palmatum
Ribbon grass	Phalaris arundinacea picta
Rose campion	Lychnis coronaria
Rose of Sharon	Hypericum calycinum
Rowan	Sorbus aucuparia
Royal fern	Osmunda regalis
Rue	Ruta graveolens
Russian vine	Polygonum baldschuanicum
Sage	Salvia
Sallow	Salix caprea
Silver birch	Betula pendula
Sloe	Prunus spinosa
Smoke Tree	Cotinus coggygria foliis purpureis
Snake-bark maple	Acer pennsylvanicum
Snakeshead	Fritillaria meleagris
Snapdragon	Antirrhinum
Snowdrop	Galanthus
Snowflake	Leucojum
Snow-in-Summer	Cerastium tomentosum
Soapwort	Saponaria
Solomon's Seal	Polygonatum multiflorum
Spanish hyacinth	Scilla campanulata
Spindle Tree	Euonymus europaea
Spotted laurel	Aucuba japonica maculata
Spruce	Picea
Stag's Horn sumach	Rhus typhina
Star of Bethlehem	Ornithogalum umbellatum

St John's Wort	Hypericum
Stonecrop	Sedum
Strawberry tree	Arbutus unedo
Sunflower	Helianthus
Sweetbriar	Rosa rubiginosa
Sweet Cecily	Myrrhis odorata
Sweet chestnut	Castanea
Sweet clover	Melilotus
Sweet flag	Acorus calamus
Sweet rocket	Hesperis matronalis
Sweet William	Dianthus barbatus
Sycamore	Acer pseudoplatanus
Tansy	Chrysanthemum vulgare
Tarragon	Artemisia dracunculus
Teasel	Dipsacus
Thrift	Armeria
Tobacco flower	Nicotiana
Traveller's Joy	Clematis vitalba
Tree of Heaven	Ailanthus altissima
Valerian, red	Centranthus
Verbena	Lippia citriodora
Veronica (shrub)	Hebe
Violet, sweet	Viola odorata
Violet willow	Salix daphnoides
Virginia creeper	Parthenocissus quinquefolia
Wallflower	Cheiranthus
Wallpepper	Sedum acre
Walnut	Juglans
Water hawthorn	Aponogeton distachyum
Weeping pear	Pyrus salicifolia
Whitebeam	Sorbus aria
Wild heliotrope	Phacelia tenacetifolia
Willow	Salix
Wintersweet	Chimonanthus praecox
Witch-hazel	Hamamelis
Woad	Isatis tinctoria
Woodruff	Asperula odorata
Yew	Taxus
Zebra rush	Scirpus zebrinus

Further Information

Baker, Margaret. *Discovering Topiary* (paperback), Shire Publications (1969)

Bartrum, Douglas. *Climbing Plants and Some Wall Shrubs*, John Gifford (1968)

Bartrum, Douglas. *Evergreens for Your Garden*, John Gifford (1967)

Benson, S. Vere. *The Observer's Book of Birds*, Frederick Warne (1960)

Boddy, Frederick A. *Foliage Plants*, David & Charles (1973)

Brownlow, Margaret. *Herbs and the Fragrant Garden*, Darton, Longman & Todd (1963)

Bush, Raymond. *Tree Fruit Growing*, Penguin (1949)

Cement and Concrete Association. *Concrete in Garden Making* (booklet), address below

Cohen, Edward. *Nestboxes* (booklet), British Trust for Ornithology

Coleman, Cyril F. *Hardy Bulbs*, Vols 1–2, Penguin (1964)

Edwards, Paul. *English Garden Ornament*, G. Bell and Son (1965)

Fish, Margery. *Ground-cover Plants*, David & Charles (1970)

Fish, Margery. *Cottage Garden Flowers*, David & Charles (1970)

Genders, Roy. *The Cottage Garden and the Old Fashioned Flowers*, Pelham Books (1969)

Hadfield, Miles. *British Trees*, Dent (1957)

Hellyer, A. G. L. *Shrubs in Colour* (illustrated by Cynthia Newsome-Taylor), W. H. & L. Collingridge (1965)

Hemphill, R. *Herbs for All Seasons*, Angus and Robertson (1973)

Hewer and Sanecki. *Practical Herb Growing*, G. Bell and Son (1969)

Hillier, H. G. *Hillier's Manual of Trees and Shrubs* (a super-catalogue), David & Charles (1972)

Hofman, Jaroslav. *Ornamental Shrubs* (illustrated by Jirina Kaplicka), Spring Books (1970)

Kerr, Jessica. *Shakespeare's Flowers* (illustrated by Anne Ophelia Dowson), Longman (1969)

Lake, F. B. *Treatment of Sick and Wounded Birds* (booklet), British Trust for Ornithology

Newman, L. Hugh. *Create a Butterfly Garden* (paperback), World's Work (1969)

Oldale, Adrienne and Peter. *Paths, Walls and Steps* (clear DIY instructions), Collins (1970)

Sanecki, Kay N. *Discovering English Gardens* (small paperback on where to see what), Shire Publications (1969)
Shewell-Cooper, W. E. *The Complete Fruit Grower*, Faber (1960)
Smith, Geoffrey. *Shrubs and Small Trees for Your Garden*, Collingridge (1973)
Soper, Tony. *The New Bird Table Book* (much wider scope than title suggests), David & Charles (1973)
Stokoe, W. J. *The Observer's Book of Butterflies*, Frederick Warne (1937)
Thomas, G. S. *Climbing Roses, Old and New*, Phoenix House (1965)
Thomas, Graham Stuart. *Old Shrub Roses*, J. M. Dent (1963)

Annual Publications concerning gardens to visit

Gardens Open to the Public, from the Organiser, The Gardeners' Sunday Organisation, White Witches, Claygate Road, Dorking, Surrey
Gardens of England and Wales open to the Public under the National Gardens Scheme, from the Organising Secretary, NGS, 57 Lower Belgrave Street, London SW1
Historic Homes, Castles and Gardens in Great Britain and Northern Ireland, Inex Publishers, from booksellers
The National Trust List of Properties, from the Secretary, 42 Queen Anne's Gate, London SW1
Ulster Gardens Scheme, from the Publicity Secretary, The National Trust, 82 Dublin Road, Belfast
Eire Gardens Scheme, from the Superintendent, Queen's Institute of District Nursing, 19 Pembroke Road, Dublin 4

Useful Addresses

The British Beekeepers Association. Mr Meyer, General Secretary, 55 Chipstead Lane, Riverhead, Sevenoaks, Kent
The British Trust for Ornithology, Beech Grove, Tring, Herts.
The Royal Society for the Protection of Birds, The Lodge, Sandy, Bedfordshire. (Approved nest-boxes and bird-feeders)
Henry Doubleday Research Association, 20 Convent Lane, Bocking, Braintree, Essex. (Useful publications: pest control without poisons etc)
Cement and Concrete Association, 52 Grosvenor Gardens, London SW1